I'll Still Be Me

I'll Still Be Me

Musical Memoirs of

Ruth Allen

authorHOUSE®

AuthorHouse™ LLC
1663 Liberty Drive
Bloomington, IN 47403
www.authorhouse.com
Phone: 1-800-839-8640

Published by AuthorHouse 04/09/2014

ISBN: 978-1-4918-5201-9 (sc)
ISBN: 978-1-4918-5193-7 (hc)
ISBN: 978-1-4918-5202-6 (e)

Library of Congress Control Number: 2014900711

This book is printed on acid-free paper.

About the Author...

Ruth Allen began her singing career in blitz ravaged London when the show went on despite the air raid warnings.

After the war, under her stage name, Ronnie Graham, she began recording as the talk of the town – the girl with the white grand piano at the chic Astor Club in Berkeley Square and touring Europe where she met Billie Holiday at the Mars Club in Paris.

When love intervened in the shape of an American GI, Ruth began a new life, a family and an enduring love affair with the USA.

But she never lost the passion to sing and write songs.
In New York, after meeting Duke Ellington, she was offered a contract by Columbia Records!
She also performed her own composition in a Royal Command performance in England, spent eight years as the resident singer/pianist at London's famous American Bar at the Savoy Hotel, and appeared, at Michael Feinstein's personal invitation, at an event he hosted at Carnegie Hall in New York.
Still recording and performing today, Ruth is also hoping to see her East End Musical "Ring Out the Bow Bells", with 18 of her original songs, on stage in the near future.

This book is a brief, factual, historical walk through a very interesting time in history. A walk through war and peace as well as sadness and happiness. The international walk of a fabulous female, occasionally in the spotlight - too often in the shadows, until now. A phenomenal singer, pianist, lyricist, composer, storyteller, glamourous entertainer, woman of the world, friend, and last, but certainly not least, my Mum (aka Ruth Allen). I am so proud of Mum and what she stands for. She has weathered every storm thrown her way and come out singing and swinging each time as she amazingly tackles a healthy 85 years young this year. I remain in awe of her beautiful smile and hopeful, youthful look, and outlook, throughout a life that's been anything but a walk in the park.

I won't give you the whole story here and now, just a few poignant points of interest–you'll have to take the walk yourself, but I will tell you that along with the twists and turns of Ruth's life, and unbeknownst to even her, a full blown 18 - song musical was born which needs to be produced and directed on Broadway (Angels, this is an All Points Bulletin— all hands on deck!!!), so there is much to do.

Mum has recently moved from the East Coast to the West Coast, grand piano and all, and is happily residing in Southern California, aka Awesome Town, for those of you that are familiar (warmer climate, better for the bones) and although she calls herself retired she gladly volunteers as a Musical Therapist at hospitals and various senior residences and, of course, is the best entertainment at all the house parties we throw or she attends.

Bring on 2014 and beyond for "Ring out the Bow Bells"!!! and remember as so eloquently written in Mum's theme song on life, "You're Never Too Old–The Trick's Not To Die Till You Do!!"

Enjoy this book and keep walking–I know I am, and if I may, I'd like to give you a small, but absolutely necessary piece of advice for navigating through this wondrous, bumpy walk of what we call life, and that is, Never be Ruthless........**Much Love Always, Beth**

1929

January 20th, fifteen minutes after mid-night I entered the world. My new parents were two marvellous thirty year olds, without a pot . . . .
One of the coldest January days in one of the coldest months ever, and my first home was a cold-water flat in Fulham. We moved from there soon after to live in my paternal Grand-mothers` house, in a street called Avalon. My maternal Grandmother lived opposite. So this then was how my parents met. There is a song called `I met my love in Avalon`, and for years I thought it was about Mum and Dad.

I started school when I was three, and could read by the time I was five. Every afternoon the little camp beds would be arranged in rows, and we would all lie down for a nap. My teacher was called Miss Griffiths and was a wonderfully gentle woman. I still remember the thrill of receiving my first library card. I was always more of a dreamer than a scholar, and I still love reading, not being very sports minded. I could high jump, having fairly long legs I suppose, but net-ball (now called basketball) did not interest me. We weren't introduced to music in school very much, only the usual. Twinkle, Twinkle, and Baa Black

Sheep kind of thing, but I, for one, did not lose out with a family like mine.

There was always music to be heard especially from the radio. We listened to the radio all the time. There were some really great shows in those years and of course all the latest songs from America. 'THE NEWS OF THE WORLD' on a Sunday would publish in full one of the latest songs. It took half a page and we would run into Gran's living room to the piano. Aunt Anna would read the music and we would all sing the song. It was a Sunday event. Most of these years I spent with my grandmother. Mother worked every day cleaning. I now know we were very poor. Music was the highlight of life at this time and I still thank God every day.

I was six years old when in 1935 my brother Alan was born, and life completely changed! Mum was besotted with having a son. (She had hoped I would be a boy). Alan became the centre of Mother's life. He was a very demanding little chap. Dad and I were almost left to fend for ourselves. I adored my Dad, and he started taking me to the theatre once a week. The Chelsea Palace was wonderful, and I loved all of it. Also the old Granville in Walham Green, now Fulham Broadway. We would sit in the Gods, with a bag of pea-nuts, shells and all, and thoroughly enjoy every minute, and all the while I must have absorbed it all. We also went to the pictures (movies) every week, sometimes twice-a-week. I loved the musicals best, and there were some great ones I remember. Snow-White was utterly amazing, and what wonderful songs. Of course Fred Astaire and Ginger Rogers made memorable musicals, and we still watch them now.

I joined a choir when I was ten and soon realised where I would rather be. I was truly happy when I was singing. It was the Band of Hope Choir, and the Choir Master was Mr. Vicary, a truly dedicated teacher and wonderful musician. I loved him, and to this day I owe to him my annunciation and phrasing. I also found I had a natural ear for harmony and perfect pitch.

The choir was extremely good and we sung in many places that were exciting, for example The Queens Hall and Alexandra Palace. I won several solo competitions there, and once all the choirs met for a most wonderful concert. Over four hundred children took part in choirs from all over the country. My family were all there and it was a day I have never forgotten.

I also took part and won medals for poetry. Little did I know then, that I would one day be writing lyrics for songs, and putting them on to C.D.s. When I look back, it is amazing to find how much belonging to that choir did for me in shaping my future. It had become a custom that every year the Choir would give a concert. It was held in the hall where we rehearsed and all our families were invited. Mr. Vicary asked me if I would sing a solo. I, of course, answered with a resounding YES! He then asked if I had a special song I would like to sing, and I said, "I would like to sing - Because".

A most beautiful song but hardly a song for an eleven-year old girl. He tried to explain that is was perhaps not suitable for me, but I begged him to let me sing it, and he did. The day arrived and my whole family came, Gran and Grandad, uncles, and aunts and cousins. When it came to my solo, I gave it my all with as much passion as I could muster. That top note was incredible, ha. Mr. Vicary glowed with pride and so did I. It was wonderful.

By this time we had moved to a much nicer place in what was then known as North Kensington. Now, it is known as Notting Hill and has become quite famous. We lived in a basement flat, in a very tall tenement. There were three floors above us. Dad had been determined to find us a better standard of living. In fact, it hadn`t been too long since these quite stately homes had had maids quarters in the upper floors. It was a whole lot different to Fulham. We had so much more room, which of course now that we had Alan we needed the extra room. We also had a garden for the first time. That was fun. Where we lived was called Maxila Gardens.

Mum and Dad had always been determined I would speak English properly the way it should be spoken. Woe betide me if I should drop an aitch. I shall always be eternally grateful to them for their care, even though it caused me ridicule at school, and some bullying, but in this area all the children spoke well, and I got on well with them.

When Alan was two and a half, we knew he was special, and destined to become a musician. He would sit with a stack of records (78s) all with the exact same label, His Masters Voice, and pick out any one you asked for. We never ever found out how he did it, but knowing now the incredible musician he is today, I am not surprised. We had an old gram-o-phone, the kind you wind up and put needles in. He started doing all this before he was two. Even when he was really ill with measles, he had to have his gram-o-phone on the bed so that he could play it all the time. As soon as he was put to bed he would start `humming` the tunes and then all the different instruments in the band, all the while keeping time by moving his head side-to-side on the pillow. Mum became quite worried that he would become brain-damaged. We should be that `brain-damaged` Ha . . . He is a consummate musician today.

I suppose I was rather a precocious child. My Mother was always telling me not to `show off`. I loved dressing up in my young aunts clothes and acting. They always encouraged me and helped me. I practically lived with them at my grand-mothers` house after Alan was born and loved every minute of it. There too was a piano. Anna, my youngest aunt, had had lessons and we would sing to her accompaniment all the songs of the day. I soon found that I could pick out tunes on my own, and somehow `knew` the harmonics of the left hand. Then again it seemed that all the aunts could strum out a tune, and would play for their partners on the numerous parties we had. My Mother was a self-taught mandolin player and Dad was a self-taught violin player. It was a truly wonderful family, and everyone could sing in tune ~!!!

Christmas was an especially wonderful time. Grandad would have gone out very late on Christmas Eve, around eleven pm, to the market where they would be selling off the leftover turkeys. The biggest birds were the last to go, and he would buy a twenty to twenty-five pound bird, (maybe even larger) for just a few shillings. Of course it would still have all its feathers on, and its head, and dear Gran would sit in the scullery with the awful smelling bird between her knees plucking the darn thing, and cleaning it. It was the most awful job, and she did it all without a single complaint. After it was really clean and stuffed with sage, onion and sausage, it was ready to cook. By now it would be well after mid-night.

It was time for Grandad to bring in the SPIT. This was a very heavy brass cylinder with a very large hook at one end, and a smaller one at the other attached to a chain, which would determine the position of the turkey. This contraption also had a very strong spring inside it, which was wound up tight. The smaller hook was then attached to the ceiling (somehow) and the turkey was fastened securely to the large hook. This was all hung in front of the old lead fire-place, and all night long it would slowly turn around and around, in front of the open fire. Gran would have covered it with strips of bacon, and a very large pan was placed beneath it to catch all the glorious juices. As I write this account I can still smell that wonderful turkey cooking.

My Grandmother always made the Christmas puddings from scratch, about two weeks before Christmas, and enough was made for all her daughters to have one to take home. They were extremely rich in content being mainly dried fruit, currants, and liberal doses of sherry and brandy. Gran would let us all know when she would be mixing them, and we would arrive to see the mixture in an enormous bowl, which we in turn would stir and make a wish. Then Gran would put in many silver charms, and separate the mixture into one big bowl, for Christmas Day, and many smaller ones. They then had to steam for six hours. When they were ready, the bowls were covered with a clean linen cloth and hung up ready for The Day.

The Day arrived, and we were all ready. All of us cousins were fed first so that we could be out of the way for the grown-ups, and their booze, Sherry usually. When we were all `stuffed` with turkey and all the trimmings, in would come the Christmas Pudding. It was set on the table; Brandy was poured on it and then set alight. The alcohol soon burned off and, at last, we were given a portion. A shout of joy would mean that someone had found a charm. Competition was fierce, but all in good fun. No-one ever choked on one, which was just as well.

In the evening it was music of course, and everyone had their own party—piece. One of the uncles, who had his own green-grocer shop, could really put over a comical song. Wonderful songs made famous by George Robey and very funny. Even my darling Gran would sing, and my fat Uncle Rupert would make us all laugh with his rendition of `AT THE DEVILS BALL`. I consider myself a very lucky girl to have had such a wonderful family. Grand-dad liked to be the star. He was a very dapper old man, with a waxed moustache, and a quiff of hair on his forehead. He had quite a good voice, and a flair for putting it over.

On Boxing Day (the day after Christmas), the entire family would go to Uncle Bill and Aunt Kits. This was the uncle that owned the green grocers. So there was always plenty of food to eat, and extras that the rest of us could not afford. Of course it always ended with everyone doing their party pieces. I could never forget those precious times.

Music was already shaping my life, I was always singing to myself, and of course the choir was my mentor. I was singled out once by Mr Vicary to go for special lessons by a singing teacher to become a contralto, but of course that would cost money, and as we didn`t have any it was out of the question. It didn`t bother me at all, and it doesn`t bother me now. The lack of funds probably did me a big favour. I became a soloist, and loved every minute of it.

Our clothes were all bought from the `Tally` man, and paid for weekly when he came to collect. I cannot remember having any new clothes; I wore the hand-me-downs from the aunts. Even when I went to central school and had to wear a uniform, it was second-hand. But no-body cared, least of all me. I still get a thrill if I find something good in the thrift shop, ha.

Poor or not, wherever we lived we were never without a piano, and happy laughter. Somehow Dad always managed to find one. It was simply unthinkable to imagine a home without a piano. But then again, in those days every home had a piano, and it seemed to me everybody could plonk out a tune. My Dads` family were also musical. He used to tell how, on a Sunday afternoon, the big treat was when his Dad brought out the old gram-o-phone, and would play the records of the day, and all the kids would sit in a circle and listen. My Grandmother had a very strong voice, and loved to sing. Grandad had the deepest voice I had ever heard, and even scared me sometimes, but he was really very kind, and was never without his clay pipe.

I had begun to wonder about my Dad. He was so different from the rest of his family. He spoke beautifully, he was incredibly smart too. One day when we were on our own, I asked him. And he was only too happy to tell me his amazing story. Apparently, as a boy, he like all the rest, had to make money for the family. His Mother had thirteen children, in poverty. She used to pawn the sheets every Monday morning for a couple of shillings, and my Grandfather's suit or anything else they might have acquired. Not all of the children survived. He told of a time when she was breast-feeding one, and watching another being carried out in a coffin. It must have been dreadful, the poverty and the ignorance. I never really knew my paternal Grandmother very well; they were unlike Mum's people. It was strange really. I said my grandmothers lived on opposite sides of the same street, and it couldn't have been more opposite. Dad's side was pretty rough. The people were poor, and in those days would be called "common". On Mum's side, the neighbours were hard workers and much more aloof.

I have no idea how this came about but it was always the same.

When Dad was old enough he had a job as a paper-boy, delivering papers in the local neighbourhood. One of his customers was a Judge. This Judge took a great liking to my father, and told his Mother that he would like to educate the boy. Of course as this was one less mouth to feed, she readily agreed. So this then was why my Dad had so much class and was so different from all his siblings. There came a time when Dad was about fifteen that the Judge decided to go to America. He wanted to take my Father with him. Once there he wanted my Dad to study to become a lawyer. Of course he had to get permission from his Mother. She said a resounding NO. He (meaning Dad) was old enough now to earn a living. He`s going to be a plumber. And that was that. I was enthralled by this story, and sad too. But then, if he had gone to America, and not met Mum, I wouldn`t be here. It must have hurt him, though he never uttered a word of complaint.

I really looked up to Dad even more. Later in his life he proved himself over and over, and became Clerk-of Works. He also wrote a book of his life, which is a work of art. A wonderful chronicle of the nineteen-hundreds.

He called it `The Passing Years`. I treasure it. I tried to have it published and though the publisher wrote to say he thought the book quite wonderful, especially the incredible account of life in the 1900s, he thought it was of greater value as a family heirloom and legacy. That it is. I still think it is a great read, and still hope one day to have it published.

1939. North Kensington.

The day before war was declared, my entire school was evacuated. We all met at the school gates. Each wearing a label with our name on, our gas-masks in their boxes slung over our shoulders, and a brown paper bag with some lunch in it. I can still `see` my Mum standing with four-year-old Alan clutching on to her hand, with all the other Mums, no one knowing where the coaches were taking their children to. As a mother myself today, I cannot imagine what they were going through. As for us kids tho` it all seemed rather a lark. I really don`t remember any tears among us. I bet there were a few shed by our families though.

Upon our arrival we were ushered into a hall, and lined up for the `to be` foster parents to choose which of us they wanted to have live with them out in the countryside. I was extremely lucky. My `foster parents were lovely. Older than my own, and with a fifteen year old daughter. Their home was delightful. I had my own room, and they had a piano in the living room. Also they lived opposite the house my best friend was allotted to. All in all it was not too bad. The very first thing my `lady` made me do was sit down and write to my Mum telling her where I was. She was very kind and thoughtful. They even owned a car, something my family never had. I thought it was wonderful. I soon became good friends with their daughter Joyce. She was very sweet and gentle. Her speech was slightly defected. She was unable to pronounce some words correctly. Mrs. Carter explained to me that Joyce had had meningitis as a young child and was very lucky to be alive. I loved her even more, even though I had never heard of meningitis. When, many years later I learned what a devastating illness it was, I was even more impressed with Joyce.

As we all know now, nothing much happened in the first three months of the war. Our school carried on in a borrowed building. My foster-parents were great, I had my pals around, and we were well taken care of. I did miss Mum and Alan though, and, of course, my Dad and when it got around to Christmas, I wanted to go home. So I did, and never returned to the country.

Dad was an air-raid warden, now, and we had moved up from the basement to the ground floor. The basement had been re-enforced with beams and the wardens used it as their base. One night when the blackout was in full swing, we were expecting company and as it was very cold, Mum had a beautiful big fire going in the living room. It was so lovely, roaring away until we heard a banging on the front door, and frantic shouts “Mrs. Berry, Mrs. Berry. Your chimneys` on fire!!” We rushed outside and there it was, blazing away like a beacon!!

In came the air-raid warden with a stirrup-pump which he shoved up the chimney, and down came the soot. When he finally got it out, and came away from the fireplace, it was too much for my Mother. She burst out laughing at the sight of him, and couldn`t stop. He was completely covered in soot and was as black as night. So was everything else. At that moment Dad arrived and was appalled. Still Mum laughed, she couldn`t help it. Then the company arrived, and seeing the state of the room, and Mum hysterical with laughter, they saw the funny side too. What a night. What a target we would have been. We had to spend the rest of the evening in the bedroom. What an incredible sense of humour my Mother had.

I shall never forget the night when Dad was out on patrol, and we heard the string of bombs coming down. One hit very close and it made one hell of a bang. We sat there wondering where Dad and his friend Mr. Banks were. It seemed to take forever til we heard them returning. They came in looking like a pair of ghosts. The bomb had landed on the local church, and they had been in a doorway opposite. They were covered in white plaster, and looked so funny we all started laughing. It broke the tension. Looking back, it was incredible how we all seemed to take it in our stride. If the siren went off during the day, and we were in school, we just got down under our desks until the ALL CLEAR blew. At home, if we had a shelter, we would go to it of course. We did have a shelter in the kitchen once. It was a huge steel box, with steel netting on the side. You put a mattress inside, and pillows and blankets. Then you all crawled inside, it. In the day-time, it doubled as a table. Truly, it was horrible. We slept in it about twice, Mum, Alan, and me. Mum had the council come and remove it, Thank God. The raids got worse and worse, and Alan, poor little boy, was so frightened. He would say, "Cross your fingers Mummy, cross your fingers". It was heartbreaking. Being a Mother myself many years later, I wondered how "they" endured it.

A shelter was being put up in the road outside. Strangely, it was built with bricks and mortar, with eye-level slits. The walls were very thick. I don`t think anyone ever used it for shelter. Us kids used to play games in it. One was to tie a thread to the door-knockers of the houses opposite the shelter, then pass them through the shelter slits, hide inside and pull the threads which would cause the knockers to bang on the doors. Out would come someone looking up and down the road. We thought this was hilarious! We`d wait until “they” had returned indoors, and then knock again. Little Horrors we were!

When we heard the wailing of the warning siren, Mum, Alan, and I, and the upstairs neighbours would all sit together in the passageway of the house. My little brother Alan always insisted on wearing an old straw hat, and wouldn`t be without it, much to everyone’s amusement. Somehow he felt safer with it. Eventually the all clear would go and we would return to bed. The raids got steadily worse.

Mother eventually couldn’t bear to see Alan so frightened, and started to take us to the underground station where many, many people were going as one of the safest places to be. At least you couldn`t hear the noise. I went with them once, with our blankets and flask of tea. There were so many people on the platform in sleeping bags and blankets trying to get comfortable. Someone had an accordion, and people were singing. I thought it was awful, Alan loved it. As a train would pull into the station he would jump on and ride up and down on the underground until he got tired and then he’d get off the train, curl up and go to sleep. I hated it, and after one time resolved never to go again. Mother continued to take Al though as long as he was happy.

I started to spend the nights with my cousin Laury. They had an Anderson shelter almost buried in the back yard. It was pretty awful but we had fun. It was situated about ten feet from the backdoor of the house, and one night we fancied some cocoa. So during a lull in the gunfire, we dashed into the kitchen. My Aunt, Laury`s Mum, soon made two cups of steaming cocoa and handed one to me. At that precise moment a bomb dropped near-by and my full cup of cocoa jumped straight up in the air, and back down again on to the saucer without spilling a drop! We immediately scrambled back into the shelter. That was a really terrible raid over Fulham. When the all-clear finally sounded we emerged from the shelter to find fires raging all around. They had hit a gas main next to a housing estate, and the flame of gas was shooting into the air for about fifty feet! Quite a sight.

In 1943 my Dad, who was forty-three, was called up. It was an awful time for Mum, I remember hearing her crying. This was something they never expected, but the government were getting very short of men to fight the war, so even men over forty were called up. So off he went. Mum didn't cry for long, but she was far from happy.

By now I was fourteen and my friend Olive and I started singing together at school. We could sing really good harmony and nearly drove Mum nuts singing the same things over and over til we got them the way we liked. Just for fun we answered an ad about auditioning for a spot in a show. We won! The big cinemas had live shows in between the movies, or pictures, as we then called them. All the big cinemas had enormous organs in those days that always played during the interval between pictures, and at the start of the programs. They were down out of sight beneath the stage.

All or our family and friends were waiting for us to appear. The Odeon Kilburn was quite the place then. Enormous and very ornate. The stage remained empty. The music swelled and suddenly our little heads began to rise from the depths with the organ. We were ON. It was wonderful. We all laughed afterwards. It was quite an auspicious beginning. Soon afterwards we were offered two weeks work to appear in a show. It was for the Trocadero, Elephant and Castle. A three thousand seater!! The show was an hour long, with costumes and everything.

Oh! The excitement. We were given three `spots` in the production. The first scene was a peacetime sea-side Pierrot show. We all wore costumes with the big bobbles down the front, and pointed hats with a matching bobble on the point. Olive and I had costumes that at first dismayed us by the shortness of the skirt. It was almost like a ballerina`s, with a sleeveless top of yellow satin, and three black bobbles down the front. We used make-up on our legs, the liquid stockings every girl wore, as we couldn`t get stockings, and glory of glories — Grease Paint. The song we sang in our own harmony was `Wishing Will Make It So`. Still a great song.

Our second spot was supposed to be a sophisticated nightclub. Olive's mum made our evening dresses. Olives was green and mine was pink satin with an over dress of the same coloured netting with a few sequins here and there. We thought they were lovely. We entered the stage from opposite sides and walked down a short stair-case to center stage, and sang You`ll Never Know`, one of the most popular songs of the day, and one of my Dads favourites— `Oh The Moonlights Fair To-night Along The Wabash`. We received great applause.

The last scene was quite spectacular. A mocked-up landing craft and as the `landing` came down—facing the audience, the entire cast walked out in every uniform of the services, with Olive and I center stage. The song we sang then was a wartime tune called `The Smiths and The Jones` and finishes with the words `We`re All Democracies Sons`. During this number around eight-o-clock every night the sirens would go . . . .  Olive and I had on army shirts and trousers and real steel helmets, which were very heavy. As we sang our heads off you felt as tho` you were sinking into the stage. We received twelve pound a week, and thought it was a fortune.

Leaving the theatre every night was quite hazardous. The nightly raids were becoming really bad, and the threat of falling shrapnel was very scary. Also as soon as the raid started the under-ground trains under the Thames would be closed, so we had to walk home, dodging into shop doorways whenever we heard the whistle of the shrapnel hurling down, or a bomb. It was said that if you could hear the whistle of a bomb, it would not hit you. One really terrible night when we were walking home, we did get scared. It seemed that the whole of London was on fire. The sky was a bright orange and we started to run. The raid was still on and we kept hearing explosions. We didn`t even speak. As we got to Stamford Bridge in the Kings Road it seemed that the incredible glow of the fires must be where we lived. But as we drew closer we could see that it was really farther back and our folks were O.K, Thank God.

Our poor Mums would be waiting on the doorsteps every night, wondering when and IF we were coming home. Sometimes when I finally arrived home my cousin Geoff would be there waiting with Mum. Geoff had polio as a child and as a result his right leg was deformed, which meant he could not join the forces, so he became an air-raid warden and would cycle over from Battersea just to be sure I arrived home all right. Of all the cousins, Geoff and I were always close. Truth to tell, I adored him. I think it was mutual. Strangely, time would prove it.

It was too much of a worry for our Mothers and as soon as our contract came to an end they made us quit. We did a few more shows later on, one good one was at the Kilburn Empire on the same bill as Ivy Benson and her all girls band. That was a good show too, and had it not been for the raids I think Olive and I would have had quite a future.

I feel I must tell you more about my Mother, before we moved to Fulham. She was a real character, a bohemian at heart, born in Chelsea, and I think could have been an artist in other circumstances. Mother had a complete irreverence to anything even if it was considered valuable, and if she should get her hands on a pot of paint, beware . . . .

We had a mahogany phonograph. A nice piece of furniture Dad picked up. It was a cabinet type, with the turn-table on the top. Mother decided it was too dark in the corner, so she painted it pea green. When I came in from school, I could not believe my eyes. Then I waited for Dad to come home . . . . He shook his head in disbelief, and tut-tutted. His look said: Lord, what next . . . . The kitchen was very small and had a very small fireplace, which was tiled in beige . . . . Not for long. Mother painted every other tile RED. It looked like a chess board. It changed colour every week after that. We never knew what to expect. Made life interesting my lovely Dad said . . . .

At this time my little Brother Alan had a small red tricycle. The living room was quite large and as was the fashion then we had a heavy oak table that stood in the middle of it. Alan would ride around and around the table at breakneck speed, and would often bash his head on the corners of it. This horrified Mother. She grabbed Dad`s big saw and to my horror, proceeded to saw all the corners off of the table. It looked awful. Then she covered it with the chenille tablecloth, which hung forlornly from each corner. That really was terrible, and Dad had a hard time not exploding. That was Mum . . . . She also had a hot temper, but as quickly as it would erupt, it was as quickly forgotten. Once, when all the grown-ups were in the pub having a drink, and it was my Dad's turn to buy a round—Dad, feeling by now a little bit merry, thought to put all the drinks on a large tray and carry them above his head (like a waiter). He started out alright but half way there, he faltered and dropped the lot . . . All eyes turned on Mum, expecting an explosion of names and more for poor Dad. However, she took it all in and burst out laughing, as did everyone else.

After Dad went into the R.A.F. Mum decided we should move back to Fulham to be near Grandma. She found a tiny house in a tiny terraced road, and from my lofty fourteen years I called it a slum and totally hated it, at first. But Mum made that `tiny` house as happy a place as you could find during a war. It had a very small back yard, and was separated from next door by a fairly high brick wall, which was the view. Not for Mum . . . she painted a beautiful blue sky, with white clouds, and beneath that, green grass and flowers. A Masterpiece! You couldn`t help loving her. The tiny space which was the kitchen, had a sink and a gas stove at right angles, and that was it. Above was a very tiny window, not even big enough to put up a curtain. Mum took a small sponge and tennis whitening, and by dabbing the sponge into the white liquid created lace, to frame the small window. Actually, it was super.

Mother was the most kind and understanding person and generous to a fault. One of my aunts was extremely attractive to the opposite sex, and was always with a new boy friend. He could be in khaki or air-force blue. An Aussie, or an American, or maybe even an Englishman, ha, who was quite often to be found asleep on the old couch in the living room. Mum would come down early and find "him". It never fazed her at all. "Hello love", she would say, "Did you sleep alright? Would you like a cup of tea?" You had to love her. She had also found a job in a bakery and used to bring home cakes and chocolates that were left over, then proceeded to give them all away., Her sense of fun was so infectious, no wonder she was always popular.

We had a party every Saturday night, a ` bring—whatever—you`ve—got,—and—as—long—as—you—could—play—something—and—sing`, party. All of us around the old piano, and anyone was welcome. We made as much noise as possible to drown out the noise of the guns and the bombs. The neighbours loved us, and would sit with their front doors open so that could hear the singing. My wonderful aunts and cousins would come and sing in three or four part harmony. They were so wonderful, and strangely enough we were happy.

Two of my young aunts, a cousin, and myself, called ourselves The Jingle Bells, a really good quartet, and we sang a few `gigs` at the local hospital and once at the workhouse. No money of course, but great fun. I think we could have made a great deal of money, if we had only known how. So much real talent and no one to guide us.

One Christmas we decided to go carol singing in the blackout, to raise money for the Red Cross. We only had our dimmed torches to see where we were going, and it was bitterly cold and we weren`t making any money either, so we decided to go into a pub. The one we chose was quite full of people, and of course a couple of us were under age. Nevertheless, we got inside and started to sing carols in perfect harmony, holding out the Red Cross tins. We collected five pounds and some, which was a great deal of money, and we were warm too. Ha. All in all we had a great time.

I had left school at fourteen and a half when we moved to Fulham and got a job as a receptionist at a Magazine company in Trafalgar Square. The Magazine was called THE COURIER. It was very prestigious, and I only got the job because my aunt Anna had it before me. She now worked at the Admiralty, a big job. I was a terrible receptionist and always cut off the bosses phone calls. He must have liked me because he sent me to telephone school for two weeks, and I came back knowing what I was doing, for the first time. The Boss was a great man, and I really loved my job. Met some super people too. Writers. I took the number eleven bus every morning to earn twenty-five shillings a week, which I gave to Mum. It was quite good then, bus fare was 1 penny and a half. Thinking back, and now knowing what a truly terrible war was raging, it was incredible how we all went about our business. Every morning I would look out of the office window (top floor) and say good morning to Admiral Nelson, ha. His statue was exactly opposite my window in Grand Buildings.

Next to singing, I loved Ballroom dancing, and when I could `borrow` a couple of bob from Mum, I would be off to the Hammersmith Palais de Danse, usually with my cousin Laury. There were always two big bands that revolved through the night one of the bands was Lou Preager, and I had such a crush on his piano player. Peter Martin. Olive came dancing with me one night, and we stopped by the bandstand and sung along with the band. Lou heard us and invited us to sing with the band (only for that one time though). It was great.

They played everything that was popular, Glen Miller, Stan Kenton. They played them all, and we danced. It was fabulous. One Saturday afternoon, I was coming home from a happy afternoon of dancing, and was walking to my Grans, where I knew Mum and my aunts always gathered for tea, when I began to be aware of piles of debris along the main road at regular intervals. Very tidy.

I turned right at the end, where I could see the `mews` entrance to Grans street, Avalon Road. There were people milling everywhere, and then I saw that the `mews` had been cordoned off. I looked down the road and there was nothing there. Where before there had been houses on either side was now nothing. A blank space. I could not see around to where Gran lived as she lived further into

Avalon. Somebody grabbed my arm and asked me if I lived down there? I mumbled no, and was told to go to the sweet-shop, they have the lists there. In a daze I got in line with my stomach starting to churn. I gazed helplessly around and wonder of wonders, I saw my Grandma with my Mum and the aunts with big bundles of `things`, walking from the other end of the street. I felt like falling to my knees to thank God. They were all just as relieved to see me.

It had been one of Hitler's latest toys, a buzz bomb. More horror. One of my aunts friends house was hit, and her father buried in the rubble. He died later, and three generations of a family who had all gathered for tea, were killed. Well this time we all went to the country for a rest from the raids. We found we had yet another aunt who just happened to own a big house in Buckinghamshire. She already had three London evacuees, but we all fitted in somehow.

Alan and I went to the same village school, which took every age in the one school. We had to walk a mile and a half to school, unless we could beg a ride on the milk cart. It was a long way for Alan at his tender age.

However, we hadn`t been there very long til one night, Mum had just put Alan to bed up stairs, I was reading in the living room, when there was the most horrendous explosion, and the ceiling was falling in upon us. Everything went hay-wire. I glimpsed Mum trying to get up the stairs to get Alan, only now they were a slope, (the stairs had disappeared). Fortunately, his room was untouched.

The evacuees were not in bed, where they were supposed to be, but in this case-Thank God. A beam had fallen right across where their little heads would have been. So by His grace no one was hurt. Apparently, a lone German bomber was on his way home with his load. This was not allowed of course, so at the first opportunity, (he may have seen a light,) he dropped the lot. The main load fell opposite aunties, and what it threw up landed on us. I was covered in plaster, just like Dad had been in London. It was so thick on my head and white. It really made a mess of her nice house too. We all had to spend the night in the one and only hotel in the village. I thought Mum would never get the darn plaster out of my hair. The next day we returned to London again and stayed there until the war's end.

The buzz-bombs made a frightful noise, but at least with them you had a little warning. When they stopped (buzzing) you had two minutes or so to take shelter. Also our gunners were getting really good at shooting them down. The next little toy sent over from Hitler was really the worst. The V2 Rockets. No warning at all, just a horrendous explosion that left you wondering where that one had landed, and who the poor devils were that got that one.

At the grand old age of fifteen, I met my first American service man. How wonderful they seemed. So glamorous, talking like our favourite film stars, smelling of Old Spice, and so well mannered. I met a` lootenant. (well that's how they said it). His name was Danny and he asked me to dance. I fell in love. He was blonde and sooo handsome. Twenty years old, and a pilot of a bomber. I told him I was eighteen, (we all lied about our age). Due to the war, we had all tended to grow up rather fast, and with make-up and so on we certainly looked older than we were.

Whenever he could he would come to London. It was all so thrilling. Eventually I had to tell him the truth about my age. He took it very well. I felt awful. Pretty soon after that, he had to return to the states. He and his sister sent me a `care package` with nylons and goodies. So kind. I will always remember him. My Mother loved him too. I think the mothers then realised that any day could be our last, and let us have much more lee-way than they would have, had there not been a war on. We all were `good` girls too, and the boys were respectful. So different from today.

At this stage of the war, everyone was tired. The V2s were very debilitating, and morale was getting low. I truly think if Hitler had brought these deadly things on sooner it would have been very different. BUT . . . . He didn`t. Thank God . . . .

V.E. day. What a day. By now almost too good to be true. I was there in Piccadilly with all the crowds. It was fantastic, and went on and on right thru` the night. No one wanted to stop partying. No more awful raids. No more buzz bombs. No more rockets. Sleeping in beds. Still rationed for a long time, but who cared. The war was over. Every street had a party. All the householders contributed something, long tables appeared from somewhere, flags appeared by magic, pianos were rolled out of someone's house, and the party began. This happened without a signal all over London. It was marvellous. The incredible relief was as tangible as a smell.

I had several different jobs for the next couple of years. I apprenticed in hairdressing under the late great Raymond. I learned so much from watching him that I seldom ever had my own hair done. I could do any style that I saw on a film star. Raymond was a hair genius. I would secretly watch him and imitate. After that I became a beautician. This was with a make-up firm and another girl and I did two weeks training, learning facial massage and how to apply make-up. I loved it. My partner was from Manchester, older than me but you would never know it. We were sent all over the place to Service-women`s camps. While one of us lectured, the other would give a volunteer a face massage, and then demonstrate a complete make-up. It was a fabulous job. The make-up was very reasonably priced for the girls and I loved it. It all came so naturally to me. My partner and I got on so well, and had so much fun in all the various places we went to. Innocent fun I might add. Her name was Edie, and she had beautiful blonde hair. I used to style it in all sorts of ways. I had a ball doing it and watching people enviously looking at her. She was a great person. It was a wonderful job and I would have continued for a long time had the next phase of my life not been looming.

Week-ends I was still dancing, and at seventeen fell in love again. He was twelve years older than me. So handsome, with the most wonderful head of hair. I soon found out he really was the Brylcreem Boy that was on a big posters everywhere. He had so much charm and a wonderful speaking voice. I was completely bowled over. So was my Mum.

Yes, Freddie really knew how to court someone he wanted. He was so much fun too. He thought nothing of hiring a Rolls Royce and picking me up in my funny little street (with all the neighbours gawping). And off we would go on a pub-crawl. Another time he hired a boat for the day, and we went for miles down the Thames, through all the locks, and stopping anywhere we liked the look of.

Oh, I thought he was the most exciting man I had ever known, said he had a flat the in the Kings Road Chelsea. So Glamorous.

It was Fred to whom I lost my virginity, lying on his coat in an old air-raid shelter in the park. The same one in which I had learned to walk. I was so dumb and naïve I really thought he loved me. Also, I was very curious. I had heard how wonderful this love-making was supposed to be from my young aunts, and the girls garbled versions at school, but I wasn`t too impressed. It hurt like hell, and made a bloody mess of his coat. It was as if he owned me after that, and I couldn`t bear to be away from him, so I gave up my super job for him. Stupid . . . . .

When I told the aunts, they were furious and wanted to tell him what they thought of him. I calmed them down and said how much I loved him. I don`t think I did, just felt that I was supposed to. When he asked me to marry him I was nineteen, and although I didn`t really want to, I thought, as I was no longer a virgin, no-one else will want me, so I said yes. Talk about green . . . . It was1948.

On our first wedding anniversary, I gave birth to a son, Paul. The Kings Road flat turned out to be a bedroom in his Mothers` house, in Kings Road Fulham. We were still living in his Mother's house and I knew I had made a terrible mistake. I became pregnant again, and when I went to my old Doctor, he was appalled. He said this man is not good. At this rate you`ll have ten kids by the time you are thirty. You must get out of this. I was scared, but I felt what the hell could I do? Six months later I gave birth to a beautiful daughter. Fred at last found us a flat. Six flights up, with two babies. It was just off Kensington High Street.

I thought I would go crazy. In those days we didn`t have disposable diapers (we called them nappies), so sometimes I was up til all hours washing the terry cloths by hand and hanging them on clothes lines across the spare room to dry. I might as well have had twins. To go shopping I had first to put Paul in the play-pen, dress Gail, and with the blanket and pillow etc, and the baby, run down the six flights, make her comfortable in the pram `which I had taken down earlier, rush back up, dress Paul and myself, and go down again. I used to take long walks with them both into Kensington Gardens, which was lovely, then reluctantly return to the prison, well — it felt like it.

After a while, I insisted on having one day a week with my Mum and he would drive me there early in the morning, and pick us up in the evening. I told no one how miserable I was. That every day I was left alone with the kids, when he wouldn`t get home till very late, usually drunk, stinking of cheap perfume, sometimes as late as two am, then wake me up to demand his `rights`. Then came the fateful day he rang to say he was sorry he couldn`t pick me up this particular Thursday as he had a meeting. Could Dad take me home? Of course he could, by bus. I had Gail who was just six months, and Dad took care of Paul who could now walk.

We walked up the six flights and found a notice on my front door — which was pad-locked. The notice said `Owing to non-payment of rent, the flat had been taken over, etc etc.' My Dad turned to me and asked if I knew anything about this. Of course I said NO. Whereupon he busted the screws out releasing the padlock, and we got inside. I fed the children and put them to bed, and then we waited for Freddie. He breezed in with ` Hi Pop, Thanks for picking them up.' Dad said, never mind that, I want to talk to you. And out they went. All I remember is the next morning we gathered up all the kids clothing, a few of my things, their baths and whatever else I could carry, and put them in the car. Then put the screws and pad-lock back in the door, and went to my Mums. We all had to sleep in her tiny front room. He went to his mothers.

My Darling Dad had bought the dining set for us, and most of the furniture in the flat.
We lost it all. Fred swore that it was all a big mistake, but by now we knew he hardly ever told the truth. I overheard him telling someone how he had just returned from Paris and what a great time he had had. He had never been out of England, Ever.

A couple of nights later he asked me to meet him at a certain pub. I took my best friend Pat and her husband with me. Fred was very drunk, as usual, and asked me to go outside and have a talk. We did. He said what do you want to do? I said I didn't care if I never saw him again. With that he hit me with such force that I banged my head on the wall and screamed. As he went to hit me again, I ducked and ran into the pub. There was an uproar. Some stranger with a car said jump in I`ll take you home. By the time we got home, I had a bump the size of a plum on my head and my face was swelling. My Mother was livid. I really think she could have killed him at that moment. So much for the charming Freddie.
Well that was the end of the so-called marriage. I took him to court for assault. Later I filed for divorce. I managed to find a good lawyer who charged me less than usual. I had a job, and I paid for it myself. It took a while. At least he

admitted the assault and adultery. Actually, he didn't have a lot of choice. My best friend Pats` husband Jim was a window cleaner, and had seen Freddie entering a house with a woman with a lot of shopping. (In fact, after a long time, he married her) Pat and Jim both came to court with me as witnesses. Such real good friends. The judge even overlooked the fact that my Dad had broken in, saying he could see the necessity of it in the circumstances. Thank-you judge . . . .

So here I was twenty-one with two kids, whom I loved so very much, and not a penny to my name. Thank God for a wonderful Mum and Dad, through that quite awful period of my life. I never got a single penny from Fred. He was too clever. A quantity surveyor (Oh he had the brains) he would always say he was out of work. Everything about divorce was so much more difficult then.

I found a few gigs singing in Men's working clubs. The toughest audience you could find and great proving grounds. One of the first ones taught me a lesson I never forgot. When I got the booking, I borrowed ten pounds and bought a very pretty evening gown, and some shoes. I looked smashing. My name was announced and I trotted on to the stage, and sat down at the piano. I sang `HARD

HEARTED HANNAH`, with a real swing. Silence. I didn`t know what to do. So I sang another song, and I can`t remember what it was, I was so frightened. Again silence —except for a small boy in the front row, who clapped. I ran off crying my heart out, vowing never to sing again.

The man who had given the job to me, and was M.C. of the show put his arms about me and apologised. He had forgotten to tell me NOT to dress up, because these people thought you were trying to be better than them, and resented you. I vowed never to return, but after awhile, I was asked back. I badly needed the two pounds (which is what they paid) so I did it. This time I wore no make-up, flat shoes, and a skirt and blouse. Did the same numbers and not only did they applaud; I had to do an encore. Hard lesson learned. Never think you are above an audience. I carried on singing whenever I could, and had my day job.

Then I answered an ad for a singing job with a band, playing at the American bases in Norfolk. I got the job and the six pound a time I asked for even tho` the band leader offered five. They were a good bunch and I loved it. We were very popular, and of course I was able to sing all the good music of the day. I would journey up from Liverpool St. and stay in a B&B in Kings Lynn with a

Mrs King. It was super. At the base, we could eat, and it was the first time I had had fried chicken. Heaven, and one time a steak that would have fed my family. Americans? I loved `em . . . .

One night at the base in Sculthorpe, the piano player didn`t show up. It looked like we would lose the gig, so I said I thought I could do it, and sing at the same time. The band leader was a bit sceptical, but rather than lose the gig he said O.K. That was the last time we ever saw the pianist. The guys loved me, and we split the extra money.

I met some wonderful people at the bases, and they were very good to me and certainly endeared me to the Americans. It was also when I became a piano-act. I could never get away from it after that.

Quite by chance, I ran into two of Freddie's friends. Two brothers who were a very good musical act. Basil and Tony. They always loved my `act`, and told me I should go to the Astor Club in Berkeley Square. They held auditions every Monday afternoon. The famous club had been taken over by Bertie Green. Tony said he would be my manager, so off we went. At first Bertie said `I don`t want a piano act, there is no piano except in the band, she can`t sit up there`. Tony persuaded him to at least listen to what I could do, even if it was on the stage. So I stepped to the piano, and did my stuff. Everyone there applauded like mad. Bertie said O.K. I`ll book her for two weeks, and they borrowed a piano from The Colony, which was next door, and I was in the West End!!.. The two guys and I danced all the way down the street.

I have forgotten to mention that a few years before all this, I had gone for a holiday with my young aunts and a cousin. While in Devon we all decided to change our names. Winnie became Wendy. Marie became Anna, Grace became Susan. And I became Ronnie, and by the time I got to the Astor I had changed Berry to Graham. Ronnie Graham. Star of the Astor Club. Wow !!

My first night arrived, and I was ready. When it came to my spot, two waiters would push the piano onto the (dance) floor, in front of the band, He put me on halfway through the show. I can`t remember who was on the bill, except the six dancers who opened the show and a beautiful girl called Diana, who did a super and classy Spanish Dance I was a smash hit. Sorry if I sound conceited, but it is true. After the fourth triumphant night, Bertie asked me to be at the club the next afternoon.

He had a car waiting and we were driven to Kensington. We stopped outside a huge piano shop. He said `Well go on in and buy yourself a piano`. Just like that. So I did! When we got back to the club, the piano arrived behind us, and the first thing that happened was a man started to spray-paint it white. They then produced some beautiful blue velvet cloth with my name in sequins on it. This was attached to the back of the piano facing the audience. Then he offered me a year's contract at twenty pounds a week as Star of the show. I was in heaven! No more worrying about money. This was more than my Dad earned. Fifty-two weeks peace of mind.

Bertie also found a gorgeous gold lame dress, with a long, long train. It had been featured in a magazine, on a beautiful model, posing beside a marble column. Well the train had to come off, and I can still relish the picture of the great Bertie Green on his knees with a pair of scissors cutting it off. Mind you, I had to pay for it weekly out of my pay. It was a perfect fit on my skinny body and in it I really began to feel like a star. Especially when I had my picture taken in it and the picture (blown up huge) was displayed in the club entrance.

Decades in the making

'Unknown' gets big Astor job

TWENTY-FOUR-YEAR-OLD girl pianist-voc[alist] Ronnie Graham (pictured above), wh[o] went along to the Astor Club for an audition [a] month ago, has proved so successful in the club floor-show that proprietor Bertie Green has give[n] her a year's contract.

Mr. Green holds auditions every Monday aft[er]noon for unknown artists. Those with anyth[ing] [illegible] to offer get engagements at the Asto[r]. Ronnie Graham is his first [illegible] discovery. She played [illegible] [illegible]

[illegible]

A Nightingale Sings . . .

"Burlington" Bertie's plush Berkeley Square niterie, The Astor, discovered this stylish vocalist, RONNIE GRAHAM. She's off now to wow them in Paris with her sultry songs at the piano.

TROUBLE IN FRENCH JAZZ PARADISE

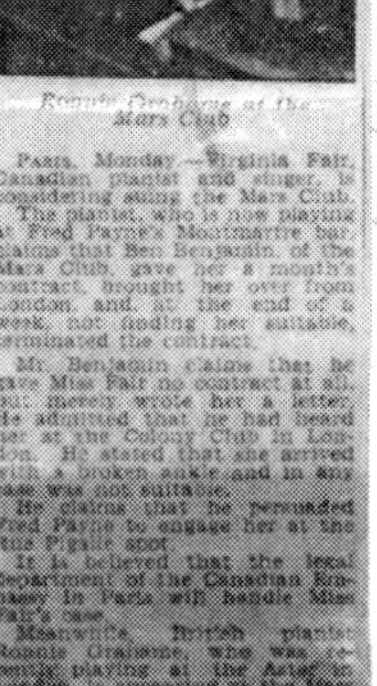

Ronnie Grahame at the Mars Club

PARIS, Monday.—Virginia Fair, Canadian pianist and singer, is considering suing the Mars Club.

The pianist, who is now playing at Fred Payne's Montmartre bar, claims that Ben Benjamin, of the Mars Club, gave her a month's contract, brought her over from London, and, at the end of a week, not finding her suitable, terminated the contract.

Mr. Benjamin claims that he gave Miss Fair no contract at all, but merely wrote her a letter. He admitted that he had heard her at the Colony Club in London. He stated that she arrived with a broken ankle and in any case was not suitable.

He claims that he persuaded Fred Payne to engage her at the Rue Pigalle spot.

It is believed that the legal department of the Canadian Embassy in Paris will handle Miss Fair's case.

Meanwhile, British pianist Ronnie Grahame, who was recently playing at the Astor in London, is appearing at the Mars Club.

Miami-bound

PRETTY Ronnie Grahame, the singer-pianist brunette [illegible] is the sweetest [illegible] her stint at the [illegible] this week and sets [illegible] to live in the [illegible]

[illegible] Her husband-of-a-[illegible] Bill Halpin of the [illegible] Air Force, has been [post]ed to Florida. Bill met Ronnie when she was leading the Astor Club cabaret. He visited the club every night of her year's stay—which must have made it a pretty expensive engagement for him! "I reckon my bills must have paid her salary," he cracked.

Ronnie hopes to do cabaret and TV in Miami and [return] here in two years' time. [Bon] voyage, lovely lady!

Barrister Bob

Latest hair style seen in London—the Barrister Bob. Here is Miss Ronnie Grahame, cabaret actress, wearing it.

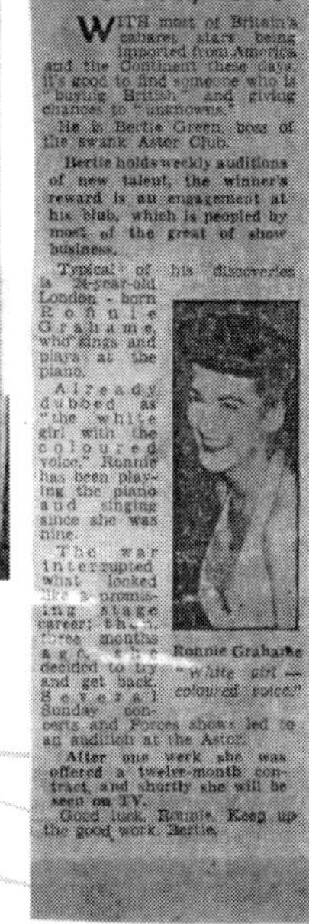

'Nice Work, Bertie

WITH most of Britain's cabaret stars being imported from America and the Continent these days, it's good to find someone who is "buying British" and giving chances to "unknowns."

He is Bertie Green, boss of the swank Astor Club.

Bertie holds weekly auditions of new talent, the winner's reward is an engagement at his club, which is peopled by most of the great of show business.

Typical of his discoveries is 24-year-old London-born Ronnie Grahame, who sings and plays at the piano.

Already dubbed as "the white girl with the coloured voice," Ronnie has been playing the piano and singing since she was nine.

The war interrupted what looked like a promising stage career; then, three months ago, she decided to try and get back. Several Sunday concerts and Forces shows led to an audition at the Astor.

After one week she was offered a twelve-month contract, and shortly she will be seen on TV.

Good luck, Ronnie. Keep up the good work, Bertie.

Ronnie Grahame "white girl — coloured voice."

Various news articles touting the talents of Ronnie Graham aka Ruth Allen

So began my great year in the west end. It was written up in all the newspapers. Unknown gets big Astor job. It was unprecedented. Every night the Cabaret started at one am. And I was the last act, and every night we were packed. I also caught the eye of a gentleman called Mr Halpern who owned another nightclub, and some nights I doubled, and played The Albany as well. I would never have been able to do all this and be with the children if I hadn`t had Mum to look after them. I had to sleep all the morning. But I was there to put them to bed.

To gain some publicity, I had to go to a theatre. I was in evening dress, and had to borrow a mink stole from Bertie`s wife. The show was `Witness for the Prosecution` by Agatha Christie. I had boasted at sometime or other that I could do anything with my hair, so they challenged me to make it look like a barristers wig. I did, and I`ll never forget hearing my Mother and Tony covering my head with silver stuff, and giggling. I didn`t know until later that Mum had almost emptied half the bottle over my scalp. It worked very well, as long as you didn`t touch it or touch somebody else, then it came off. It really looked as though I was wearing a wig. Well it made the Evening Standard. "Miss Ronnie Graham, seen in London wearing the Barrister Bob.

About half way through my contract, I knew something was wrong with Mum. She was not at all well, and kept getting palpitations. It was the menopause. I had to find someone else to take care of the kids. I found a woman called Mary who took care of kids from show-biz people. She lived in Balham in a real nice home, and she agreed to take Paul and Gail for me. It was one of the hardest things I`ve ever had to do. Even tho` they were well cared for, and well fed, clean and everything, I hated it. I could only visit them once a month as Mary said it upset them too much if I went more often. But I really had no choice, and I was able to buy them things. Nice clothes and toys.

It lasted about six months until Mum was on a medicine that made her feel like her old self. She wanted the kids back, and Oh God so did I. It was so good to have them home, and pretty soon Paul started school. He soon adapted, and Gail had her Nan all to herself.

Meanwhile, ha, back at the club, things were going great. Backstage the girls were such fun, always gossiping about their boyfriends and so on. Then they began talking about an American who came in very often, and always sat in the same seat. We would take turns peeking thru` the dressing room curtain. He was really nice looking and very serious. After a while he would smile as I left to go home. Then one night he stood up and asked me if I would have a drink with him. To my own surprise I said yes. That was the start of an affair. His name was Bill. The first thing I had told him was that I had two kids, but it didn`t seem to put him off at all. He was everything Fred was not. Kind and gentle. I finally found what real love making was all about, and it was very wonderful.

An American Officer whose name was Major Gherkin was in one night to see the show. He was the head of the U.S.O. shows in Germany, and was on the lookout for talent. He thought the whole cabaret was perfect to put on tour of the American Bases for six weeks. It all sounded pretty good. We were all to be paid the same amount each week, and pick up the rest of our pay when we returned. Diana and I became very good friends and roomed together. In Stuttgaart, we met up with the Major, who took us for a meal and asked us how we were getting along. Somehow, the conversation got around to what we were being paid, I mean the full amount. We told him and found out that actually we should have been getting double. Too late, we had all accepted the contract. But the greedy Mr Green lost out because he never got another show booked.

Astor Club Revue October 1954

Astor Club * Revue

Ol' Man Me plays and sings in a manner very reminiscent of Louis Armstrong.

Bertie Green's Astor Club Revue, direct from London's Astor Club, is touring Germany for U.S. service personnel during October, November and December under auspices of the European Armed Forces Professional Entertainment Division. Headlining the Astor Club Revue are the Astor Girls, four dancing beauties, and Ronnie Graham, of radio and television fame. Diana Montel is a Spanish and Hawaiian dancer. A lively dance team, The Courtneys, do the Acro Adagio dance. England's Louis Armstrong, "Ol' Man Me," does a sensational trumpet and singing act. The master of ceremonies and comedian is Gary (Slim) Allen. Musical accompaniment is provided by the Astor Club Trio. Itinerary for the revue: Oct. 27, Dillingen; Oct. 28, Leipheim; Oct. 30-31, Ulm; Nov. 2, Neubiberg; Nov. 4, Fuerstenfeldbruck; Nov. 6, Straubing; Nov. 7, Oberammergau; Nov. 8, Augsburg; Nov. 9, Dachau; Nov. 10, Landshut; Nov. 11, Augsburg; Nov. 13, Murnau; Nov. 14, Fuessen; Nov. 15, Freising; Nov. 16, Munich; Nov. 18-25, Nurnberg; Nov. 27-28, Heidelberg; Nov. 29, Karlsruhe; Nov. 30, Kaefertal (Mannheim); and Dec. 2, Karlsruhe.

Diana Montel, Spanish dancer, also does an exciting hula.

The four Astor Girls are a charming and versatile group.

The acrobatic Courtneys are a Command Performance ...

Above, the Astor Club Revue principals surround Maj Fred Gerken, European Armed Forces Professional Entertainment Division Director (standing, center). Bertie Green, owner of the Astor Club in London is third from left.

Right, Ronnie Graham, radio and TV star in England, brings down the houses with clever songs. —S&S by Doherty

Ronnie Graham
Radio and TV star in England

It took a while for my Mum to forgive me for going to Germany. She thought it was awful, after what they had put us thru`. It was hard to convince her we were doing it for the American boys.

A French couple, also on the lookout for a new act found me at the Astor and wanted to book me for their club in Paris. Bertie did not want me to go, and I practically had to beg him. I really needed to get away and at last he allowed me to go.

The Club was called the Mars Club, and was quite famous, (I learned). Many famous artistes had played there, and all had their names put on the door. Now mine would be added. I soon realised I was a bit out of my depth to be playing for such long periods, instead of the cabaret. The hours of work were 10pm till 4am! Seven nights a week. but at 24years, I could handle it. At around one—o—clock you had difficulty seeing across the room. Everyone smoked those Galoise and it was like looking thru` grey chiffon.

I was saved by the resident pianist, Art Simmons, who was absolutely fabulous. He could play anything. I started to stand up and sing with him, and we became almost an act. We had tremendous rapport, and I was thrilled to bits. He taught me some new songs and I was in music heaven. All the artistes in town came to check me out, and they were all wonderful to me. One night there was a great buzz going around. The famous Billy Holiday was paying the club a visit. I felt so ignorant. I had never heard of her. Art soon put me in the picture, so by the time she and her entourage arrived I was in awe. She listened for a while, and then got up to sing with Art. I had never heard anything quite like it. She sang a song called ` Strange Fruit `. I thought it was so sad. After the club closed that night she invited Art and me to `dinner`. It was incredible. And unforgettable . . . . That was 1954. One of the men in Billie`s entourage who wore black-framed glasses, just kept snapping photographs all the time. If there was any film in the camera, there are pictures of Billie and Art and me somewhere . . . .

Also during that same month, I was asked if I would take part in a March of Dimes show in Lyons. There were a number of artistes working in Paris going, so of course I said yes. Among them was Charlie Beale who, like Art, was a super piano-player and accompanied the show. Misha Auwor, a most strange looking American comedian, was the Star. It was quite an adventure. While in Paris, a friend took me to the left bank one afternoon to hear some incredible jazz in a cave. You literally had to duck your head to get in. I had never seen anything like it, or heard anything like the music. Mostly black American musicians, the leader was Bix Beiderbeck on soprano sax. There were so many black American musicians at that time. It was a place they could be themselves without the feeling of any racism in France and a freedom to play their own kind of jazz that was truly appreciated. That month in Paris was a wonderful learning experience for me and one that stood me in good stead for the years ahead.

I returned to London to finish out my contract around Christmas. By now Bill had received his orders to return to the States, so Bill and I were married on December 28th, in London, with Paul and Gail and Mum and Dad and all my friends. I should have said Bill was in the U.S. Navy at this time so he was in uniform, and so was his best man. As my first marriage had been in a registrar in Fulham, this time it was in a church, and blessed by an American Vicar in Kings Wiegh House Church in London. My dear friend made my wedding dress. It was off—white velvet, cocktail length and quite lovely. I made a heart shaped hat to go with it. The reception was in our apartment, and Bertie and some of the cabaret came, and my other boss Mr Halpern, and all our friends.

In February, we set sail for New York. The name of the ship was The Geiger and it was supposed to be its last voyage. I hoped it was mine too. I would never fancy cruising . . .

Saying Good-bye to my parents had been terribly painful. I hadn`t realised HOW.

The crossing was one of the roughest on record, even the crew thought so. My darling daughter was sooo sick, she couldn`t stand up at all. Paul was fine and had a great time. It took six awful days to get there, and by the time New York and the Statue of Liberty was in view, and Bill was telling me to look I couldn’t have cared less. We got our baggage and car and went to Detroit so the kids and I could meet his Mother.

When I had told Fred that I was getting married and taking the children to the States, I had to get him to sign papers saying that my new husband was adopting them. He signed without ever wanting to see them again. Thank God they were too young to know, and hadn`t seen enough of him anyway.

Meeting Bill`s folks was fine. His Mum was very kind to my kids. He had six brothers and sisters, so she was well used to dealing with little ones. Gail was able to eat again, and the family made us very welcome.

Bills` next assignment was Key West Florida. The car ride over that ocean highway was amazing and a little scary. Only two lanes, one going and one coming. No room for mistakes, and it was 157miles long.

We found a very nice apartment where we could live until we could got Navy accommodation. One night, I was alone, having just put the kids to bed, and about to clean up the kitchen, when I saw what I thought was a `daddy-long-legs` coming up from behind the sink. I was about to put the big box of cereal away, when the rest of `his` body appeared, IT WAS HUGE!!. The biggest bug I had ever seen. Somehow it scrambled up into the cereal box and I shut the box as a reflex action. I ran out of the back door and banged on my neighbours door. She happened to be a Captains wife and very nice. She took one look at my face and pulled me inside. (She later told me I was green). I sobbed out my story, and she told me I could stay until Bill got home. I really didn`t want to go back into that house, but of course I had to, and if we were going to live in Key West I would have to get used to bugs as there were an awful lot of them. All different kinds, and all huge. Some could fly. From then on I hated the place. The children were playing outside one day when I heard screaming. Gail had sat on a red ants nest, and was covered in the horrible things. Bill rushed out and grabbed her and put her straight into the shower, but she was badly bitten. I hated the place even more. I didn't know how much more of this heart stopping stuff I could take, but a lot more was to come.

We were given a house on the base-housing, and they were pretty awful. Four units in a row. Ours was an end unit. Soon we found out there was no getting rid of bugs. Before moving in Bill had fumigated the place. Well the evening we moved in, upon opening the back door, the floor was alive with an assortment of bugs. Bill started stamping on as many as he could in some crazy looking dance. I just sat down and cried, especially because Bill was on night duty, and I would be left alone with the two kids and a million bugs.

We later learned that whenever you fumigated your house they just moved on to the next one and so on. You could never get rid of them. Mosquitoes were as big as houseflies, and I found out I was very allergic to them. It was absolute misery.

There was a communal yard in back of the house safe from traffic. One of my aunts visited us for a few days with her husband and daughter, Paula (who was a year or so older that my Paul). He worked for Shell Oil, and they were stationed in Venezuela. It was wonderful having them. The kids had been all playing outside when Paul came running in white as a sheet, and saying that Gail was in a hole. We all rushed out and there was no sign of her, but Paula (their cousin) was standing crying and looking down. Bill ran over and looked down too. There was Gail on a ledge down a sewer, trapped by the manhole cover that had fallen in with her on it. My aunt's husband and Bill, both big fellows leaned in to get her out. By some miracle she was unhurt, tho` we rushed her to hospital just to make sure. If she hadn`t been trapped she could have fallen to the bottom and been swept out to sea. It took both of these big men to put that manhole back where it belonged. How those three little kids managed to move it we never found out. Another year's growth gone.

It wasn`t long before I found a club down town and started working. I guess I was a bit of a novelty, and everyone seemed to like me. There were some good artistes in town too, and we quickly made a lot of friends. It was incredibly hot all the while, and in the July, we were listening to a guy playing piano when I passed out. Sunstroke, they said.

By the way I was a very slim size 10. I felt O.K. until it happened again and Bill took me to the base hospital. A very nice Docter examined me and told me I was four and a half months pregnant.

Everything had been normal due to the change of climate etc. The next day, I let it all hang out. A friend said she had never seen anyone get pregnant so fast in her life. Wonderful, a four and a half month pregnancy. I had the most beautiful little boy on December 17th. 1955. We named him Greg. I don`t recommend anyone getting pregnant in that dreadful heat, and then I insisted on cooking Christmas dinner, English style, in 90degrees. Bill was pulling every string he could think of to get us out of there, and when Greg was six months old he did it.

A posting to England. I was euphoric. Only it was by sea. We had to go to New York again. We stayed at a hotel for service personnel, the room was like a dorm and. After the kids were in bed we were pretty much in the dark. Bill had to go to the Brooklyn Navel yard to get his pay, also pick up Greg's` passport. Somebody in Key West had fouled up, and he couldn`t get paid and Greg's` passport still hadn`t come thru. We were broke, and stuck. July is no place to be stuck in a hotel room with three kids and no air-conditioning.

Bill started working in the coffee shop washing dishes etc. so that we could eat. His Dad sent us a little money, and the Red Cross sent a little too. It was over a week before the passport arrived, but by now the bloody ship had sailed. Bill, resourceful as ever, got us a flight on an air force plane; I think it was held together with chewing gum. It made the most terrible noises, and groans, but the kids slept, and we were FLYING HOME . . .

We all finally arrived at my Mothers. Oh the excitement! It was so wonderful to see them both. Paul and Gail were over the moon, and how they loved Greg. He really was the most lovable of babies and so good-natured. Bill was to be stationed at Bushey Park, and the kids were to go to the American school there. A bus picked them up every morning. It was a long way, but they didn`t seem to mind. By now we had a flat in West London. Another dump but all we could afford. I was home, I didn`t care. I was so glad that my parents had met Greg, and loved him.

The year went by so quickly. Not much music either. Then once again it was time to return to the States. Another awful farewell and good-bye. We flew to New York, and then to Detroit. Of course, Bills Mum and Dad were over the moon to meet their new grandson, and to see all of us again. At this point Bill decided to change to the Air Force, as he could not advance any more in the Navy. It was strange to see him in an air-force uniform but it suited him. Our next port of call was Cape Cod Mass.

It was a beautiful place and right away we rented a charming little furnished cottage not far from the water. And wonder of wonders it even had a piano! I loved it, but no sooner had we settled than Bill had to go away to school for four months. In the next cottage was another air-force family, and I had to rely on her to take me shopping on the base. I hated having to rely on someone else . . . .

Our car sat in the driveway, and I decided I have to learn to drive. After the older kids had left for school I would take Greg, who would stand beside me on the front bench seat, with his arms stretched along the back of the seat. And off we would go, slowly. I should have said this was after the summer visitors had left, and the place was virtually deserted. I would drive around and around, occasionally running over a small bush, at which time Greg would say `Watcha doin` Mum'. I told no one especially Bill, hoping to surprise him.

Around November, we had a terrific snowstorm. It howled all night we were almost buried in an enormous snowdrift. I shall never forget opening the front door and being confronted by a white wall from top to bottom. The kids thought it was hilarious. Then we found there was no water. I filled the kettle with snow to make a cup of tea, and wondered what the hell to do. About the middle of the morning I heard a shout, and there were people outside, digging us out, and that was how I met two life-long friends, the best people ever. Actually we had been cut off for two days.

Their names were Marion and Fred. As soon as I came to know them better, I told them of my driving adventures, and Fred volunteered to take me out driving while Marion minded Greg. Her youngest was about Greg's` age, and they used to play together. Eventually, he deemed I was ready to take the test. This took place in Hyannis. I passed the first time! I was one proud lady. Marion with her three and I with mine took them all to Plymouth for the day. It was great. Marion and Fred introduced me to all their friends, who were really great people, and as soon as they found out I played the piano, we had parties every Saturday night. I was in my element. Such good fun. They brought all the food and the beer.

When he came home at last, Bill was so impressed with my driving license and with all the new friends I had made. We had a party for him too.

I had my eye on a super ranch-style house that was for sale. Bill liked it too. Somehow we bought it, and moved in. On a corner lot, with woods behind it, it was lovely, and had a full basement. We were in a lot of debt; I think three mortgages at one time. But being young we managed to find some furniture, and a piano, ha, and settled in. Greg was a little slow in speaking English. He had a language all his own. Sometimes rattling off long sentences. Gail, who adored him, was the interpreter. I`d listen to try and decipher what he was saying, finally giving up and asking her, "What did he say"? And she would say he wants a cookie, two or three. He would get his cookies, and be perfectly happy.

It came as a bit of a shock while we were living in the town of Falmouth, that to my dismay, there was a Jewish restriction in the town. I had also heard of a hotel that had recently opened. It was called the Seacrest Hotel and Beach, strictly for Jewish people. A Mr. Mohr from New York had bought up a sizable chunk of beach and put this super hotel on it. In the summertime, it seems most of New York pours into Cape Cod, so the place fills up to capacity. Smart man Mr. Mohr, and Mrs. Mohr, of course. I applied for a job as a cocktail pianist, and got it. Ten weeks of work, and well paid. We would be able to catch up on our debts.

It was 1958, and things were great. Greg had suddenly started speaking perfect English overnight, and had a wonderful sense of humour. Far beyond his two years of age, and was a constant source of amusement. Whenever he became tired, he would come in and say, "I`m gonna take a nap Mum", grab his constant companion, an old blanket, curl up on the couch and promptly go to sleep. Sometimes he would lie down outside on the grass, and I would find him there, usually with a couple of dogs asleep around him.

One day I had a call from the hotel. A guest had a special party on. Would I go in early to play for them. More money, sure I would, and as luck would have it Bill was home for the evening to baby-sit. It was August and a beautiful evening. Bill had Greg in his arms to come and see me off in the driveway. Greg swung away from his Dad to hug my neck, I kissed them both. Said bye to Gail and Paul and off I went, all dolled up for the job.

The cocktail party went off very well, and before I had to start my real job, I sat down and had a light salad with the band-boys. They were always good for a laugh. I looked up and suddenly saw our friend Tom coming into the room. The first thing I noticed was he was wearing his old work clothes, and I wondered why, he would ever come in to the hotel looking like that, as I got up to greet him. He had a strange look on his nice face as he haltingly told me that Greg had been run over by a speeding car. I felt as tho` I had become numb all over. He said Greg was all right he thought. I was already moving. The band-boys had heard, and stood in shock.

Tom's car seemed to take forever going to Hyannis Hospital. I could not think or speak only to keep saying Please God No. Not Greg, Please not Greg . . . . . .
We finally got to the hospital. My legs didn`t want to work. Tom had my arm and together we entered into a hallway. Bill was walking away from us, Tom called and he turned.

He said, “He didn`t make it Ron”, and I collapsed. I don`t remember going home or anything else that dreadful night. Tom’s wife had gathered Paul and Gail up and taken them to her house. Bill took me home. I was in shock and disbelief. I kept thinking I must go with Greg, but I didn`t know how. I thought, he is only a little boy, he won`t know where to go. I must go to. It fell to Bill to phone the grandparents.

Visitors, in their kindness kept arriving at the house, until a couple I had never seen before started praying over us, and I erupted . . . . How dare they try to tell us how to behave. GET OUT, I shouted and literally threw them out. I was beside myself.

I learned later, that the night it happened, Mr Mohr cancelled the band and dancing, and the next day we found a tea-chest full of food on the doorstep, from the Hotel. They were so kind and showed us so much respect. Everybody did. Bill`s parents arrived, and we had a Memorial at the base chapel. Then Bill and I, and Greg, in a small white velvet coffin, were flown in an air-force plane, with so many flowers to Washing D.C. to Arlington National Cemetery, where our beloved son was buried in Military style, with two young airmen carrying him. This is where, when Bill dies, he will join his son.

I really don`t remember the flight back. Paul and Gail were waiting for us, at home and my dear friends had removed Greg's` crib and all his toys. It did seem to make things a little easier to bear. We proceeded to try and get back to normal. Paul came to me one day shortly after and said, "Mummy, where is your smiley face? You've still got me". I hugged him and hugged him. From then on, I really made the effort to recover. Bill had even more of a burden to endure blaming himself for what happened.

It appears that one of those ice-cream vans, with the jingly music, had come along and of course all the kids rushed out to flock around it. All of us who lived there all year round, seeing the `van` and knowing there would be a lot of kids around, always slowed right down, before proceeding. We always had ice cream in the house, so our kids had no money. They joined the others anyway. Greg apparently decided to go back and stepped from behind the van. A car driven by a young summer visitor was talking to her companion and driving too fast, failed to notice him. He landed seventy yards down the road. To this day, I can`t stand the sound of those vans. I forgave whoever it was that killed my son, although we never received any kind of message from her or her family. But nevertheless, she has had to live with it all her life, like us.

I remember one particular night, Bill and I had talked and talked. No way did I blame him, but he took some convincing, and crying together, we made love as never before. It was such a needing of each other, and we poured in to one another. I was convinced that I had conceived. . I counted the months and days, and concluded that I would give birth on May 9th 1959. And I did . . . . The healing had begun.

Just after I had Beth, and because we needed a night out, we got a baby-sitter. Bill had heard that the great Duke Ellington and his band were appearing at the N.C.O. Club. It was almost too good to be true. We had so many of his recordings, and had to see him. The concert was absolutely marvellous, and in the interval I said I HAD to meet the great man.

We went back-stage, and there he was. We started saying how much we were enjoying his music, and he asked me what I did. I said, “I`m a singer”. He said, “Come and sing with my band”. Honestly . . . . And, then I said, and I still can`t believe I actually said it, “No Mr Ellington, thank-you. I`ve had a couple of beers and I might make a mistake”. He looked at me and said, “Well I think you really can sing, and here is what you do. Don`t deal with the middlemen. Make a good demo, and take it to my producer in New York, his name is Irving Townsend". The Duke never got to hear me sing a note.

I went to Boston, and made the demo. Three songs. My neighbour took care of the kids, and Bill drove me to New York, and Columbia Studios. We met Mr Townsend, who was most charming. However the accompanist who was to play for me did not show up. Bill said, "Play for yourself". So once again I did. It was a huge studio, with the biggest grand piano I had ever seen! The technicians sat in a glass box above the room. I had never felt so alone. A disembodied voice suddenly said, "O.K. Miss Graham", and I was on. I finished the first song, (which in those days was put straight on to acetate) and the voice said, "Can we hear another one please". I sang again til I had sung the three songs I had prepared. Still the voice said, "Another one please". I was now relaxed and having fun, and so I ended up practically making an L.P.

Finally Mr Townsend appeared. He said my voice was great. Better than Jo Stafford, but they couldn`t sell any of their stars. Doris Day, Peggy Lee, and to promote someone like me would mean I would have to travel the entire U.S. on tour. I thought of my tiny new baby and said, "Out of the question", and that, as they say, was that.

The next Christmas and for four years after that I received a Christmas card from Duke Ellington. What a truly great man, musician, and Gentleman.

Unfortunately it was 1959. The start of Rock and Roll. My timing was really OFF. And it never improved much either, except in my music, of course.

Beth had arrived on May 9th, as I had predicted, and it was like giving birth to Greg all over again. She was the same child. Big blue eyes, dimple in the chin, same weight. The only thing missing was his tassel! We were so happy, except Paul, who had wanted a brother. She was followed the next year by her sister Lynn who weighed in at five and a half pounds. She was also the longest baby I had ever seen. Twenty one inches, and the only brown-eyed child I have ha. Lynn too, had a real head of dark hair. I couldn`t get over the length of her legs though. Even today she has difficulty buying trousers. The two of them were a real handful, and quickly grew up.

In 1962 Bill received orders to England. We could hardly believe it. We were to be stationed at Sculthorpe, in Norfolk. It was the best news ever. I hadn`t seen my folks for five long and eventful years. Now they were about to meet their new granddaughters. All through the years

I was away from England, Mum had sent me the Daily Mirror, a week's worth at a time, wrapped in brown paper. How I loved those papers.

Dad met us at the airport, and he was shaking all over. Oh, how good it was to see him. The `tiny` street where we had been through so much had been demolished, because of war damage, and Mum and Dad had been re-housed in a flat. They hated it, but had little choice. It wasn`t too bad, and it was home . . . . Paul and Gail were elated to be with their beloved Nan and Grandad, and the little girls were spoiled a lot. They looked a lot like twins by now, and I had made them some cute clothes.

For almost a year we lived in a hotel that had been taken over by the American Air Force. It was pretty dreadful, called The Glebe, but eventually Bill found us a bungalow not far from the beach in Huntstanton, a beautiful sea-side town with a great beach. Lots of sand dunes. The road leading to it was full of large potholes and we nicknamed it Miscarriage Drive. The bungalow was in a village called Holme Next The Sea. We moved in during the "off" season. It was quite remote. The older two kids were picked up for school, and Bill worked ten-hour days on the base.

I kept sane, left with two monosyllabic babes, with the aid of L.P.s. of Ella Fitzgerald, Sarah Vaughn, Peggy Lee, Rosie Clooney, etc . . . . I would put 12 of them on and let `em go. No wonder then, that when in the future I would need a huge repertoire, it was all there stored in my head. All the Cole Porter songs and Gershwin and Irving Berlin. I didn`t realise it then but that year was invaluable to me. We had no T.V. there but didn`t miss it either. We had a sun room that ran the length of the house where the kids could play even when it rained. I loved it there actually, but of course the time came when our name came up for housing on the base.

This too was O.K. The houses were well furnished. It was a good assignment. I began to get gigs at the clubs N.C.O. and the Officers Club. It was funny to think of the different circumstances I sang at these places all those years ago and made lots of new friends. The first Christmas, Mum and Dad came to stay with us, it was wonderful, and we had a great party, like old times. They were going to stay over Boxing Day too, but the weather forecast a huge snowstorm, so they got the train back to London. We didn`t see the ground again til March. What a winter that was. Unbelievable. I developed a "female" problem that resulted in my having two DNCs. The result being that on our return to the States I had to have a hysterectomy. Having had five children I didn`t mind a bit, and it cleared everything up too.

Our next assignment was to a place I had only ever heard of in Westerns. Utah . . . . It could have been the moon. Again we lived on the base. The houses were more than adequate, and interestingly, I had a French `wife` living on either side of me. We, of course all had kids, who quickly made friends. That is one good feature about all the moving around. So once again we settled down. Bill was flying those flying gas-tanks, where they re-fuel fighter planes in mid-air, and he was gone much of the time.

I joined the Music Union, and a trio. They called themselves the Scotsmen. Don`t ask. We started getting lots of work in the various hotels and clubs. Soon I was doing solo work as well. Utah is anything but sophisticated, but we found an audience that enjoyed `good` music. We auditioned for a new club called Intrigue. The night we arrived at the club, it was still being painted. We met the owners, Bob and Marvel Davis. I felt an immediate rapport with these two wonderful people. Once again a friendship that would last a lifetime.

Sadly, Bob was killed instantly when his car was obliterated by a concrete mixer. Marvel asked me to sing his favourite song at his funeral, the one he always requested whenever and wherever he came to hear me sing. Funny Valentine. It was one of the hardest things I have ever done, and I could not sing that song again for a very long time. Marvel was left with four kids, and we became her extended family.

By this time Alan, my brother, was fast becoming a great jazz pianist, and writer. He began sending tapes of his tunes, which were very, very good. One I particularly liked I found myself humming all the time. We were stuck indoors one weekend, because Bill was on alert. Which meant that any moment a very loud bell, which was situated above the front door, RANG— and he had to be on the flight line in three minutes. It was the same in every house and drove us all nuts.

I was idly thinking, Oh who needs spring anyway, and in that moment I had found a title for Alan`s tune. I proceeded to write `WHO NEEDS SPRING` the whole lyric, and indeed became a lyric writer. We have since written many songs but that will always be a favourite. It turned out to be a love song. Alan proceeded to send me more tunes and I wrote the lyrics. One is Hip, Hip Hooray, a fun song with a terrific swing. It came to me so easily, but if you asked me where from, I would have to say I don't know. I find that listening to my brother's lovely tunes I can hear the lyric I need in my head. It all just seems to come together. Funny thing is Alan and I never had the chance to become close as friends, or brother and sister even, but in our music we had a built-in understanding that is fabulous . . . meant to be . . .

Bill had always promised me to return to England when he retired. That coincided with Gail`s graduation and he kept his promise.

This time we found a wonderful house in Palmers Green. By now the little girls were really growing up. We hadn`t been there a day when Beth went missing. I was frantic, and the man who lived next door heard me yelling her name and informed me that Beth had gone to the nearby park tad-poling. After a while here all the kids came home carrying a bath between them with all these tadpoles in it. I was so relieved I forgot to be angry.

Anyway, it was great place, and could visit the folks by bus anytime I wanted. Paul worked near-by, in an electrical shop and Gail worked in London. Bill got a job in a warehouse on the American base. The family next door were so nice and the kids all got along well. Beth and Lynn went to the local school, and found they were well able to blend in. It was great. It was also the arrival of `the MiniSkirt`. When Gail first bought one, and I saw my beautiful young daughter in this short, short skirt, I nearly had a fit (it also made me feel so old). When My Mother saw it though, she thought it was wonderful. Ha, I never could bring myself to wear one though.

I kept thinking how I would love to stay there. Maybe buy the house. It was great location, with the lovely park at the end of the road, and shops just around the corner, and of course a ride away from Mum, Dad and Alan. Bill on the other hand couldn`t wait to get back to the States. There was a terrible war going on in a place we had never heard of, and as the year was coming to an end, and we would be returning to the States, my son Paul decided he would enlist in the U.S. Navy. He had made up his mind. It was the time when I had to tell him and Gail that Bill was their step-dad and that he had adopted them. Wow . . . .

They wanted to know all about their real dad. Was he still alive? I told them as much as was necessary. They seemed pleased. I never told them the real truth. Wait til they were older and wiser, I thought.

To my dismay Bill decided we should go back to Utah. I was pleased at the prospect of seeing Marvel and all my friends there,— but! Once again the Air-force shipped us back and there we were Utah . . . . We found a nice house, with a full sized basement, and once again settled down. Paul was in San Diego, and eventually assigned to a Cruiser called The Jupitor. It sailed to North Vietnam.

I became a volunteer at the geriatric hospital in the district. Every Thursday I would go and give the dear old folks a sing-a-long, and they really loved it. I also worked another day as a volunteer and became President of the Auxillary. I loved that year, and worked hard, and received my thousand hour pin, for service. I still have it. I was there for six years, even when I was a school teacher's aide. I realized then how therapeutic music is. The musical afternoons were such a success. One day I asked if anyone could play an instrument, and one dear man said he had a squeeze box. So I asked his sister to find it and bring it in. When he proudly came in with it on Thursday, and said "I can play anything as long as it's in the key of C" we had a ball. Another lovely lady had a beautiful voice, and whenever we hit a bit of a lull, she would say, "When in doubt sing Springtime In The Rockies", and we did.

I soon got in touch with the musicians I knew, and started getting gigs. The kids went to the local school. This was the sixties and Gail was in the middle of it. So Gail and her best friend Robyn moved to California with their boyfriends (who were in a band). I can only say I was envious. They were so attractive and wonderful, and it all seemed so innocent. They were happy too—I didn`t worry too much, and they turned out fine.

The little girls went to the local elementary school, and when Lynn was in 3rd. grade the teacher asked if the children knew anyone who could help putting on a musical show for Christmas. Lynn`s hand shot up. "My Mum can do that", she said. That was how I landed a full time teachers aide job that was to last six school years. I loved it and found that I could produce shows that were really good. I loved the children, and they loved me. My main job was in first grade and I found it so rewarding, and the more I had to do the better I liked it.

Bill decided to go to College on his veterans grant. I must admit I was jealous. I had been deprived of an education, because of the war. It hadn`t worried me at the time but as I grew older, I realised what I had missed, and it gave me a bit of an inferiority complex whenever I was around well educated people. I was always well read and could converse with the best of them, on most subjects too. But it was always there inside me.

So it was a bit ludicrous really that here I was with no credentials, being treated like a teacher, (by proving I could do it) and my husband going to college. I was very glad for him though` as he was enjoying it.

Twenty years in the service hadn`t prepared Bill for the real world, and he had a hard time finding anything he wanted to do, but college seemed to suit him, and he was enjoying the campus life. I was not so sure. I didn`t know this side of Bill. Something of him seemed to leave me. He had to study of course, but he never shared any of it with me, or told me what he was studying. He shared it with a graduate. Was it just jealousy I felt? I really don`t know, but I felt we were growing in different directions. He never came to one of my shows at my school, and it hurt.

Then we heard from my Mother that Dad had had a coronary and was in the hospital. I suddenly realised how damned far away we were. The girls were already in their teens. I got the first flight out. Dad was O.K., Thank God. When I was sure he was all right I returned to Utah, but it alerted me to the fact that my folks were getting on, and the time would come when . . . . Which in the nature of things, happened.

Dad was now seriously ill in hospital. I went home again. The journey to the hospital was dreadful. Two changes of buses, and it was bitter cold. I feared for Mum. Alan was away on a cruise playing with a trio. I was talking on the phone to one of the aunts, and said, "Doesn`t anyone in this family have a car?" and she said, "Well Geoff does and he`s bought a house not too far from your Mum". Geoff? Cousin Geoff? She gave me the number.

I called and he answered. He was at the door in 10 minutes flat. We hadn`t set eyes on each other for twenty-five years. It was incredible. He looked just the same. I had put on weight, but we couldn`t stop looking at each other. He had never married, and had just finished decorating and furnishing the house he had bought. A three bed-room duplex in a beautiful avenue in Worcester Park. He drove Mum and me to visit Dad, and they were so glad to see him. Dad had always been very fond of Geoff as a boy, and recognised what a brilliant lad he was.

After that, I knew if I was to find real happiness, I had to make the hardest decision I would ever have to make. Dad had bone cancer of the spine. It was only" a matter of time, and not very long. I owed it to them to be there for Mum too. It was truly an awful time. I now knew where I really wanted to be, and it wasn`t Utah.

So after twenty-one years of marriage, most of it happy, it had to end. I needed my life back. I went back to the States, and told Bill I wanted a divorce. It was traumatic. When I told Beth and Lynn Beth said, "What took you so long?" I was amazed. I hadn`t realised how perceptive she had become. Lynn was very upset. I found a strength I didn't know I possessed. Everything just kept falling into place. I felt it was right. Even the divorce came through in record time, and once again I flew to England. Dad died in October 1975.

Geoff took me to his lovely house, opened the door, and said, "Everything I have is yours." and he meant every word. I started living with him. I missed the girls terribly, and had nightmares every night. Although Geoff loved me with all his heart, and I him, it was never to be consummated. Geoff had been a bachelor all his life, and his up-bringing had been quite religious. He had absolutely no need for sex. In fact he thought the whole idea was messy. At first I was secretly appalled, and had fantasized about Bill. In that respect we had always been most compatible. I must admit, I missed making love dreadfully. But I was surrounded by love of a very different kind, and it was beautiful. It took a long while, but gradually I became used to it.

By this time Paul had finished his four years in the Navy, and had settled in San Diego. He had changed. He had hated the war, when his ship had sat off the coast of North Viet Nam and bombarded the shore. All he could think of was who was on the receiving end, with whom he had no quarrel whatsoever? It hurt him, and left its mark. Being a very gentle soul, and living simply.

In 1976 I went to California to visit Gail. She had a most wonderful apartment and we always had a lot of fun together. We had persuaded Paul to drive up from San Diego and stay with us, and we also had a couple of friends visiting. Kendal and Barry. Barry's Mother called and invited all of us to a Benefit Show at the Santa Monica Auditorium. As it was a Sunday evening with nothing much to do we all said, might as well. We arrived to find hundreds of cars and people everywhere. There was a long red carpet leading to the entrance. Thinking WOW, this must be a really big benefit; we slowly made our way to the carpet. Suddenly, in the entrance Barry's Mother appeared. She was a very attractive lady, and she was waving us to come forward. Feeling quite superior we sailed up the red carpet to meet her.

She led us all inside and to a bar where we all were given a drink and then she proceeded to show us to our seats. The auditorium was enormous, and we had seats in the "circle" overlooking the ground floor which was entirely made up of huge circular tables filled with people. Quite a sight especially when on looking closer I saw Lucille Ball and Desi Arnaz. Then we all started seeing STARS everywhere! The place was full of BIG STARS! Even saw James Cagney. So thrilling and this was just the audience! We still didn't know who was in the show.

Well, it turned out to be the greatest show any of us could ever have hoped to see. Head-lining was Frank Sinatra and all the so called Rat Pack—Sammy Davis, Dean Martin, Joey Bishop, and Peter Lawford. The Orchestra was led by Henry Mancini. There was Jo Stafford and her husband, Paul Weston. Milton Berle and Johnny Carson. The most incredible line-up anyone could ever see. And there we were, thanks to a wonderfully generous lady, who never gave us a hint of what we were about to see. To me, to be there with Paul and Gail was unbelievable, and unforgettable.

On a visit to California, Gail and I stayed with him, and the day before I returned home he said, "Mum, whenever a Sunday comes around, and wherever I am, I know you will be cooking a roast. It is my security. So, this time I am going to cook YOU roast beef and yorkshire pudding!" He did, and it was truly wonderful. As Gail and I were leaving San Diego to return to L.A. he leaned into the car and said, "I love you Mum" I remember thinking, God, I thank you for giving me such beautiful kids.

I returned to England, and started thinking what I would do. I had to work. Before leaving my school in Utah, the Principle had given me a letter of introduction, stating that I had extraordinary expertise with children, etc . . . I was very touched. Anyway I saw an ad asking for a kindergarten teacher at a private school. I had to work, and I wasn`t ready to sing so I went for an interview, and got the job.

Oh, how different it was to the American school I had just left, where everything was to hand. This was an English Prep School for boys, Called Arundel House and every thought and lesson had to be invented. An old Victorian house and as cold as an ice box. The boys were four and a half, going on five. In one year with me they had to learn to read, learn their multiplication tables up to three, and learn to add, subtract and multiply. What a challenge, and just what I needed at this time. They also had to learn how to tie their shoes, use scissors, and greet people properly.

They wore uniforms. Short grey trousers, white shirts with red and blue ties, dark red blazers and caps. They had to raise their caps whenever they said good morning or good afternoon, etc . . . . Every night I devised ways to help them learn, and Geoff was marvellous. He came up with such great and innovative ideas. And teach them I did.
When Christmas came around the Head Master said I didn`t have to bother putting together a program as I was just starting. Well . . . I decided I would love to be bothered . . . .

I had a piano in my classroom, the biggest room, where assembly was held every morning. The room had one small gas-fire in this enormous room and the little boys' knees were blue. I played the hymns every morning, before class. I had sixteen boys and loved every one of them. They were marvellous, and I taught them some American Christmas songs, with actions. Geoff made me some belts out of black shiny cardboard with big gold shiny buckles. I made pointy hats of red crepe paper with white bobbles on the top and green crepe pointy collars, like elves. I turned their blazers back to front, put on the belts, and they looked wonderful. Incidentally, I had been told there was no money for costumes. Ha.

Well, need I say, my little guys brought the house down! Little did they know they were singing Peggy Lees rendition of Here Comes Santa. It was a riot. I stayed at the school til the end of the year and my little darlings passed into the next class called transition. There were only four teachers at the school, and four classes, then they would "graduate" and move on to the next school. Unfortunately I had to leave as the enrollment was down. Those dear little boys had healed me sufficiently and I wanted to sing again. Their respective Mothers` presented me with two silver matching cups and an enormous bouquet. I cried. One of the teachers who had been there for fifteen years said she had never seen anything like it.

—

When I first went to the U.S.A. I had been surprised to learn that there was a male artiste called Ronnie Graham, who was a great writer and piano-player. It made me think, especially when, on turning up for a gig, I found out that "they" were expecting a man. A might disconcerting. So, when I felt ready to start singing and performing again I decided to change my name. To let go of the past, as they would say today. I had to re-invent myself. I had been christened Eileen Ruth, and as I said before, changed my name to Ronnie. Ruth was always my favourite name and I wish it had been my first name. So I became Ruth. Geoff's second name was Alan, (like my brothers) and I changed the spelling to Allen, and there was the new me. I liked it. RUTH ALLEN.

Through different people whom I had met by now, I had a network of "friends" in the business and was getting quite a lot of work. One night when I was playing in the Champagne Bar in Curzon Street, two girls who had been passing heard me singing and came in to see who was making music. Here I met a wonderful woman who is still my dearest friend, and has been a faithful fan ever since. She herself had been a dancer with the well known BlueBell Girls in Paris and before that, at the famous Windmill Theatre in London (the theatre that never closed all through the war). She was married to an actor, though divorced by the time we met. We have such a great friendship and always will. Her name is Jacqui.

Then I moved onto The Chelsea Hotel in Knightsbridge. The piano lounge was on the first floor and situated beside a swimming pool. It was kind of strange but a nice atmosphere. I only ever saw someone actually swimming once. Oh, except at a "posh" wedding reception. Everything was going great, and they were all enjoying themselves, requesting songs, etc. when one of the men guests dressed in a dark red velvet suit, jumped into the pool fully dressed. I was shocked. Then some of the others followed. I thought, how stupid can you get, but the waiters took it all in their stride.

One night I had just finished at midnight and some friends asked me to have a drink. They were sitting beside the pool so I joined them. We were chatting away and having fun when I looked up and saw my Geoff come in. I said `Look there`s Geoff come to drive me home. (I usually got a taxi). I ran over to him, and immediately saw something was very wrong. He had great difficulty talking then he told me Gail had called from California to tell us that Paul had been killed in a car accident. I couldn`t take it in at first, and then I collapsed. Surely life couldn`t be that cruel. But it was.

I had only seen him and Gail two weeks before when he had cooked Sunday lunch.

Geoff drove me home, we were both crying. I couldn`t believe it, and kept thinking there must be some mistake. It was too terrible to comprehend. My beloved Paul. Why did God want my sons ?? We got home and had to start calling the family. The next morning we went to my Mothers. Poor Mum almost collapsed as well. My aunt and uncle came over to the house, as did my dear friends. I drank a whole bottle of scotch, and no one tried to stop me. I stayed completely sober. I could not deaden my mind, which kept screaming WHY? WHY? WHY?

The two girls flew to California to be with Gail. Gail was a tower of strength. I couldn`t make the journey. It was impossible. Throughout the service I had the phone to my ear. Paul had been attending Palomar College with his Navy grant and had made so many friends who were devastated. He was taking, drama, and English etc. The night before he had produced and directed GODSPELL, to great acclaim. Paul had often called his sister frail Gail, but she was anything but frail now. She showed a strength we never knew she had. Not only her beloved brother, but her best friend had gone. Paul had always said he would only marry when he could find a girl he loved as much as his sister. Yet here she was taking care of him at this most dreadful time. I had his ashes sent back to England, where he was born, to join his Grandad.

Once again I was under contract; Once again I was on a gig when someone had come to tell me about my son. It was so unjust. But once again music came to my rescue. I had to carry on. After two weeks I returned to work. Turned my mind off and did it. I cried every night at home, but that was my time . . . .

Quite some time later Gail had found some of Paul's writings. Poems and stories. There was among them an essay that he had done for his College class. It was dated two weeks before he was killed and the teacher had given him an A. The title of the essay was "Death". Gail believed he knew what was about to happen. We'll never really know of course, but it somehow comforted us . . . . The essay was brilliant, not gloomy at all, but quite profound. When my Mother died at 87 years I had it read at her funeral service. She would have been so proud.

Eventually, I became strong enough with Geoff's` help, to help me live with the grief. He was so good for me. He was a photographic re-toucher and air-brush artist, very much in demand with Ad agencies. He had a studio at the top of the house, where he worked every day .By now it was January, as a matter of fact, and my birthday. We had had a light sprinkling of snow. I heard him calling my name and running down the stairs, shouting, "Look at this, look at this!" His hands were closed together and as he opened them, lying there was a beautiful butterfly, Alive, in January! Where on earth had it come from? A beautiful Monarch butterfly. It flew out of his hands into the kitchen. I rushed to get the camera as it landed on the windowsill.

A thought came from out of no-where. This was a present from my Paul for my birthday. The butterfly lived for ten days. We would rush down every morning to look for it, till the day it was no longer there and we never found any remains. But it lived in my mind and I wrote my best song, words and music called, “JANUARY BUTTERFLY.” After it was finished I realised it was almost an analogy of my own life. I later read in a book about butterflies, that a tribe of Indians believed that butterflies were the souls of children. This was 1978. Exactly twenty years (and the same month) since Greg was killed.

I received a call from an agent who offered me a stint in Spain. It was to open a new bar called Bloody Mary, which I thought was rather funny, and the contract was for two months. Full board. Geoff and I discussed it and thought it would be just the thing for me and give me a chance to work out some new material. The fact that I could not speak Spanish apparently did not matter.

So off I went with the agent for the grand opening. The piano was a sight to behold. A full sized grand, with wooden pedals that were more like paddles! It was so out of tune, it was barely playable. Two months!!! My mind was screaming. The `boss, a very small man, assured me a man was arriving from somewhere to tune it. I thought `Good Luck`.

I was taken to my apartment in a high-rise block, two blocks from the Bar. Wall to wall bed, and a bathroom, with a two burner stove in the nook, sorry, kitchen. The good thing was it had a super balcony. No television, no telephone. I wasn`t too sure I could do it. However, I started playing opening night and a number of English people turned up. The grapevine was very powerful in these parts. We all ended up having a good time. The place was quite opulent, for a small seaside town about fifteen miles from Almaria. The bathroom was in onyx and black, Very Swish.

The days were long and hot. If it had not been for the balcony I wouldn`t have survived. Every night I would dress in full evening dress, and sail down to the club in all my glory. And every night there would be a line of elderly gents lining the route, ha, who would clap as I went by murmuring Muy Bueno. It was amazing. Then the families would come in. Mother, Father and maybe six children, stand around the piano and stare at me for a while, then silently file out. I don`t think they had ever seen a piano, let alone some female playing one.

One happy note was a jazz club right next door, and when I quit playing, around two am, I would stop in to unwind and listen to some jazz. The guys were good too, and I sometimes sang with them. One night around three o clock, I walked "home:" and into the elevator to go to the fifth floor. It started to go up and then stopped. It was pitch dark, the elevators being situated in the centre of the building. It was such a shock that I had an out of body experience. It was as if I shot up to the ceiling and looked down at myself, standing there in my long black evening dress. The elevator was only big enough for four people. I felt down the wall and found the top of the door half way down, and there in the centre was the small window near the floor. I took off my shoe and started to pound on it. I thought this is what it feels like to be buried alive!

The bedrooms were all on the outside of the building so no one could hear me. After a while I sat on the floor and started singing Somewhere Over The Rainbow at the top of my voice. Suddenly I saw a flickering light visible through the half of the window, and then a foreign voice said, "Root-ees that youuu?" I screamed YES . . . It was a German girl who loved the Bloody Mary, and had often been in to hear me. She said she would go and find the manager, and started going away, with the light. Once again I was plunged into darkness. The manager finally came with two other people and opened the door, and I leaped out into waiting arms, quite forgetting there was a gaping hole underneath me. The power cut lasted until eleven the next morning. I sat on the balcony watching the lights of the cars on the highway, drinking brandy . . . .

I was so happy to end that contract, even though they asked me to stay another month. I had met some lovely people and made some new friends, but I was eager now to play in London. Another call from the same agent who said to go to a beautiful restaurant called The Arlington for an audition. And so I met wonderful Mike MacKenzie. He was the resident performer there and was looking for someone to replace him while he went on holiday. He chose me. I had six wonderful weeks there and also made a very precious friend. Whenever Mike went away after that I was his deputy. That restaurant is now called The Caprice. Mike was London's answer to Bobby Short in New York. A wonderful entertainer. It was very flattering to follow him.

I next went to Sweden where I toured the hotel circuit for nearly three years. I loved the Swedish people. They are very musical. I was still having bouts of awful depression, and there was a church in Knorshopping, quite near the hotel. I went in and heard the singing. The tears started streaming down my face and I could not stop crying. People stared but I didn`t care. When I eventually calmed down, I felt so much better. I guess I had been keeping it all in too long. I befriended a Swedish family of whom I became especially fond. The daughter, Anna, was only thirteen when I first met them with her brother Jonas, eleven. Their Mother invited me to their home, and to show my appreciation, I volunteered to cook them all a Sunday dinner. Roast beef and Yorkshire pudding. I bought all the ingredients in the local market.

The kitchen was super and I loved the custom of always lighting a candle to welcome a guest. I put the beef on to roast, did the potatoes and veg, and then proceeded to mix the batter for the Yorkshire pudding. When it was in the oven we went into the living room to have a drink. Anna kept running back to the kitchen to look through the glass door of the oven and see how the "pud" was getting on. Her Mother Marion couldn't understand how the thing would rise without baking powder or yeast. I assured her it would. Anna would come back and say, "It's not doing anything" several times. I was getting very nervous, and silently prayed it would RISE. My prayers were answered and up rose the best Yorkshire Pudding I have ever made! Triumph! They all enjoyed it very much. They were such lovely people, and I felt like I had known them all my life. We stayed friends for a long time, and they even came to London and visited us.

I learned much later their daughter Anna died of heart disease at twenty-two. I was shattered. She was so beautiful. She had been married six months.

One of the best gigs in Sweden was Malmo, at the St. Jorgan Hotel and I got it! I really had some great times there. The two bar tenders in the piano bar were gay and so wonderful to me. I loved them both. Bert and Kayey. After my first night when I had eaten in the restaurant before playing they invited me to join them in the charming room behind the bar. I was delighted and every night after, I ate with them. They were so gracious. The table was always set so beautifully. It was wonderful. One Saturday night during a break Bert asked me if I had ever been to Copenhagen, and when I answered no, he suggested we should catch the ferry and go on Sunday morning, have lunch on the ferry.

The slow ferry took about an hour and a half, so lunch (silver service) was a leisurely affair and quite elegant. Bert ordered schnapps for us followed by a beer. Heady stuff. We drank the drink and ordered lunch. Another schnapps appeared. "Did you order another one?" Bert said. "No". I said. We looked out into the room and saw a smiling man holding his glass and raising it to us. Bert said, "I don't know whether he fancies me or you darling but drink up and smile." We did. By the time dinner was over we were pickled . . . . Never did see much of Copenhagen. It was hilarious and so much fun.

Another time Bert asked me had I ever been to a gay club. Having been told NO he said he and Kayey would like to take me. I'm always up for a new adventure so after work on the Saturday at around 1am we arrive at the club. It was within walking distance from the Hotel. My first impression was incredulity at the beauty of all the people. I couldn't stop staring. We found a table and the boys ordered wine. I had my back to the room, and was facing Bert. I suddenly heard him say quietly to Kay, "Oh my God here comes Peter". I couldn't see "Peter" but felt him pat my shoulder and ask me to dance. I turned around and almost died of shock. There stood, all six foot of him, the most gorgeous long-haired blonde, wearing a turquoise satin leotard, with a black boa, black fish net stockings, and high heels. As offhand as I could I said sure and giving Bert a raised eye look, I took to the dance floor, but not before Bert muttered, "God I hope he doesn't fall out of his leotard." What a night.

I also met a wonderful, charming man who would come to the bar every night. His name was Burya Sundman. He had a wonderful face. The kind you wish you could paint, so full of character. He had been through a lot having been widowed twice. He became a good friend.

Actually, he wanted to marry me, so being very shy he got his best friend to ask me. I, of course, was taken. We had some hilarious lunches in a French restaurant. He had a great sense of humour. I wrote a song for him when I returned home, and recorded it, The Lonely Man of Malmo.

In Gothenberg I met up with a band. We had awful digs in the same block. If it hadn't been for them I would have gone home. The Manager of the place was so awful. We all hated him. I was suffering another bout of depression and was on a bus one day going to the hotel. My arm was resting on the ledge of the window. I was fighting back tears and dropped my arm into my lap, and right there, where my arm had been someone had carved a name—Paul . . . I felt he was there with me. I immediately felt a surge of strength. It was incredible and beautiful. I could go on.

Stockholm was beautiful. I had two wonderful months there. I loved the old quarter and on my night off would go there and listen to the jazz, it had so much charm and the people were so friendly. By now I was tiring of touring and wanted to get to work in London again, and Geoff. I blessed him every day for his unselfishness and understanding. A truly great partner. So it was back to London. I had learned so much from travelling and meeting so many different people, and would never regret it. However my travelling days were far from over.

My youngest daughter Lynn called to tell me she was getting married. Like me she was nineteen. I had managed to get to all the kids graduations. Wouldn`t miss it for the world. I think I could have owned a plane by now for all the thousands of miles I have flown, and am still flying. The marriage was fine, though I didn`t like her intended, he didn`t seem good enough for my Lynn. Meeting her father there was strange, I felt as if I still wanted to hug him, but didn`t dare.

I was there for Lynn, too, when after three years she gave me my first grandson. Trevor. Then when he was a year old I had them come to our home. Geoff was great with the baby. Unfortunately, her marriage did not last. Like Mother???

I started my next contract at the Britannia Hotel as resident pianist, five nights a week. Eight till twelve. We had a tough time making it work, but when we did it became the place to go, especially on Friday nights. You would have thought it was a private club. Sometimes the people were six deep around the piano. We had so much fun. Here again I met some extraordinary people. I learned secrets, saw all sorts of liaisons—I also was the most discreet piano player in the City. Ha.

Observing the nightlife from behind a grand piano is to say the least, illuminating. Lone men tell you all their troubles, come in with their wife one night, then with their mistress (and a knowing wink) at me, on another night. One wealthy financier had a blonde bimbo and spent a fortune on her. Minks and sables diamonds you name it she had it. He had a suite in the hotel, and was in every night.

We knew what she was up to but the poor man was besotted. He overheard me telling a friend that my daughter Beth was to appear in cabaret in L.A. and how I wish I could be there. The next night he came in alone and told me what he had overheard, and said, "I think that you should be there, and I'd like to arrange a flight for you. You have given me so much joy through your music, please let me do this for you." It was almost unbelievable. At his insistence, I went to Los Angeles for the weekend, and saw my darling Beth performing at a place called The Rose Tatoo. I was so proud of her and she was great.

During the years I was at The Britannia (thirteen years in all) I wrote a musical. I never dreamed that I could, but I did. It started when I heard my brother playing a beautiful tune, I hadn`t heard before. He had written it, of course, and I loved it. I started to write a lyric about a middle-aged couple who fell in love. It became a song called In Love. I started singing it and it seemed that every time I did someone would come up and ask me what show it was from. Set me thinking.

Of course the middle-aged couple was Geoff and me, but I couldn`t go there. Then something happened that I can`t explain. I had been asleep and dreaming when suddenly I saw a newspaper's big bold headlines: `THE BARROW BOY AND THE HOOKER`. It was still with me as I woke up. Later I suddenly realised that I'd found my middle-aged couple, however bizarre it may seem. My mind seemed to take off. I was writing a cockney Musical. I had been reading about St. Mary Le Bow, the famous church in Cheapside and how you were only a true cockney if you were born within the sound of its distinctive bells.

The characters poured into my mind, and with them new songs. Every Friday night "the gang" would crowd around the piano-bar, and I would try out the current new song for their approval. It was so wonderful. Pretty soon the "girls" would sing along with me and so became "The Ruthettes". It was a riot. And when my beautiful daughters would visit they would sing with me in the most perfect harmony. They were great nights, and the bar manager whose name was Norberto, known to all as Nobby, was wonderful.

The Musical is called `RING OUT THE BOW BELLS`, and is also the title of the opening number. I belong to a professional club in London, called the C.A.A. It stands for Concert Artistes Association, and when I told them, their reaction was "Why don`t we put it on?" So we did, those who took part were fabulous. I loved them all so much. They all worked so hard. The hall was full to capacity. A great friend of mine was entertaining an American gentleman, and he saw the show, and loved it. We could only put it on for two nights and he insisted on coming both nights. Then said "Find a producer and I`ll put money into it". Well we tried and tried, but it was always the same old story. I was unknown as a writer, and my name wasn`t A.L. Webber. Etc., etc., etc

While my life revolved around the hotel every night, my days revolved around Geoff. I loved to watch him working. His incredible skill at re-touching photographs was amazing. You should have seen some of those famous models before he removed all the flaws. I was asked to "open" a new studio in Fleet street, that Geoff did a lot of work for, so I wrote a song all about the things I had watched him do. It`s called, "He Never Retouches Me". He thought it was "brilliant". I have performed it many times since, and it always makes people laugh.

STREWTH! LUMME DAY! COR BLIMEY O'REILLY! WHAT A TURN UP! IT'S ONLY THE EAST END PREMIERE OF...

Ring out the Bow Bells

Charity Concert Performances of
Ruth Allen's Cockney Musical at
St Mary Le Bow Church, Cheapside
23 & 24 June 2008 Tickets £20

Book your seats now on 07957 364 216 and support
St Mary Le Bow Young Homeless, Wingate Golden Oldies
and the Three Score Club

Gail decided that she was fed up with L.A. and wanted to come to England to live. As she had been born here, it was no trouble, as she had never become an American citizen. It was simply wonderful to have one of my kids close. She is a very talented portrait artist, and I am so very proud of her. Geoff loved her too, as he did all the girls.

Sitting at the piano early one evening I heard, “Are you Ruth Allen?” I looked up to see a strange rather large man sitting at the piano-bar. “Yes”, I said. He introduced himself as Don and said, “Friend of mine gave me one of your tapes” (I’d forgotten to mention that while working on the continent, I was asked to make tapes of myself that many people bought). He went on, “I think you are just what I have been looking for. I would like to be your publisher”. I nearly fell off the stool. He thought I wrote in the footsteps of Porter and Gershwin etc. BUT original!

It was a few years later when the album, “The Ruth Allen Song Book” came along. I was so proud! We had the cream of London musicians and twenty strings on four of my songs. It took two days to complete. Two of the most exciting days I had ever known. To hear my songs arranged so beautifully and played by these very talented musicians was more than I had ever dreamed possible. One of the songs I especially had written for Don was called “You Took The Time”. As he had taken the time to listen. A lost art . . . .

THE GANG THAT SANG

HEART OF MY HEART

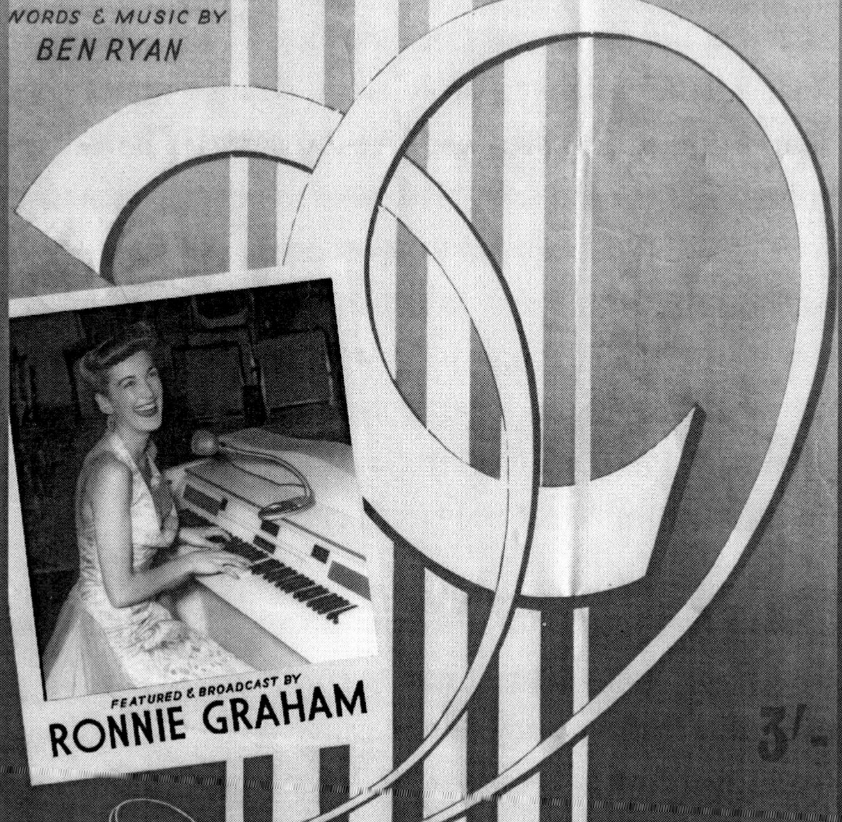

R. A. F.

Royal Airforce Broadcast 1954

The Britannia introduced me to some wonderful people over the years. I befriended a young beautiful actress who used to stop in to listen when she was nearby. She, in turn, introduced me to a playwright friend of hers, Trevor Handoll. As we talked in between songs he asked me whether I ever played for charity. I replied, of course, and he then asked if I would perform in Birmingham, expenses only. Yes I said. He assured me it was for a good cause. Then he said could I possibly write an original song for the show. Apparently he had written a sketch, and wanted a song to go with it.

He described the sketch about a soldier returning home after the war. Hadn't seen his wife and kids for years. They lived up north. I loved the idea and asked a man who had had the experience, "What was your first thought when you arrived home?" and his reply was "Thank God we all survived." I wrote a song called `NOTHINGS CHANGED`. When I gave him the tape I had made of the song he was delighted and wanted me to meet a Colonel friend at the Chelsea Barracks. I thought it strange but went along. We had lunch at the Barracks, and the Colonel had listened to my song and thought it was wonderful.

I was then introduced to his little company of actors and we started rehearsing the sketch with the music. I had written the song as being sung by the returning soldier, but found to my amazement that he wanted me to sing it, and explained how it would work. So of course I went along with it. The weekend of the show arrived. We were to travel up to Birmingham on the Saturday, stay in a hotel overnight, for the performance on Sunday. It was 1985. On the way up I said to Trevor, "This must be a pretty big show." (he had been mysterious about telling me anything about it). I asked him who else was taking part. He casually said, "Well there`s the cast of Hi de Hi, and Billy Dainty, and Sir Harry Secombe Alfred Marks . . . . At that point I stopped him and said, "this is really a big show isn`t it?" He replied, "Well actually, it`s a Royal Variety Show at the Birmingham Hippodrome." I about fainted . . . .

Ruth Allen appearing in a Royal Variety Show! It was for The Army Benevolent Fund, in the presence of Her Royal Highness Princess Anne. Colonel-In-Chief. On Sunday afternoon we had a "band call." Everyone to the theatre for a run through. I sat in the audience and watched Sir Harry Secombe rehearse. It was amazing. After a while I heard someone call my name, and up on the vast stage I went. The orchestra had my music that had been arranged by Basil Elms. I had never even met him, but he had called me at home and explained the arrangement he had done of "Nothings` Changed". At the enormous grand piano, I was to sing the verse ad lib; the orchestra would then come in behind me. It was so thrilling. All those wonderful musicians and the leader Frank Renton. It was wonderful, and when I had finished singing they all stood up and applauded! I guess my song was the only piece of original music in the show, among the "Blue Birds" and the "We'll Meet Again." . . . . The show was called OH! WHAT A LOVELY PEACE.

The Show was absolutely wonderful. Sir Harry actually said to me that it was the best Royal Variety Show he had ever taken part in. Unfortunately, and sadly, it was not taped or videoed. We all lined up to meet the Princess in person and she was very gracious. What a night to remember, and if I hadn`t been playing at the good old Britannia, it would never have happened to me.

I finally decided to leave the Britannia. It was a wrench, especially leaving Nobby, of whom I was very fond. Him, and his lovely wife and family. Seemed like we were all a great big family. I had heard that Mike MacKenzie might be leaving London to live in Spain. He was suffering from arthritis and had been very ill. After twenty-five years in the West End he was always the top entertainer.

Royal Variety Show 1985

Oh What a Lovely Peace - Birmingham Hippodrome

When the call came asking me would I like to play the Savoy I was very happy to say yes. However, I really couldn't play every night any more. It was too tiring with the journey on the train going up and the taxi ride home. I had had enough. So they asked if I could play three nights a week, and I accepted it. I stayed eight years. The other half of the week a great friend and wonderful performer Baz Norton played. We became a great team.

Again, when all was going well, my darling Geoff became ill. It soon became apparent it was cancer. He was operated on and we kept our fingers crossed. In the hospital he contracted the MRSA bug. He seemed fine for almost a year, and then the cancer came back. Another operation, then a third, and each time he was put in isolation because of the MRSA bug. The third operation was botched. I have never seen anybody in so much pain and sheer agony as my poor darling was. It was misery-I felt so helpless. He had chemo and radiation, and I swear the radiation microwaved him inside. It was horrific. I took care of him at home until the last three days of his life and then he went into a hospice, where he died two days later.

We had finally become man and wife in1991, just a formality really, and at the insistence of his dear Mother, my aunt Flo. She was so happy he did the "right thing".

His Dad had passed on awhile before. Aunt Flo was such a lovely lady, I had always loved her. While Geoff was himself ill, she passed away. I am so glad she didn't have to witness his dreadful suffering.

Geoff endured dying for two awful long years. All his friends attended his funeral and I am sure some thought it was strange, but he insisted he didn't want anyone saying anything. We just had our favourite music playing. The incredible background music from "SOMEWHERE IN TIME". It was so appropriate, emotive and atmospheric. He would have loved it. Whenever I hear it now it comforts me. I miss him so much. His ashes joined my son Paul, as will mine when the time comes. That was 1997. We had been together twenty-one years and married for six. He left me everything. That was a love like no other . . . .

In August 2000 Lynn gave birth to another boy, Jordan. She still lives in Utah. It was all rather a shock so long after Trevor, but Trevor is a man on his own now, and Lynn is loving having a little one around again. I am delighted to have another grandson. I think he is definitely going to be musical too. Ha

The Savoy asked me to play for the Millenium, and as Beth was spending Christmas with me I thought we would have a ball. It was the BEST! . . . . I didn`t have The American Bar that night, they moved me to another room. One overlooking the Thames River. What JOY. We had the best view of all for all the fireworks and everything. What a marvellous night out of many.

I was still playing at The Savoy and hating going home to an empty house. That is the worst part. One night, about six months after I had lost Geoff, I met a man. It was on a Friday night. He was rather distinctive, well dressed, and in his seventies, I guessed. Completely bald, which I personally do not find attractive, but that`s just me, I guess. He was seated at the back of the room, but as the evening passed he moved forward until he was right beside me.

We exchanged pleasantries, said his name was Richard, and he requested, `Midnight Sun`. I was impressed. I knew the song and sang it, to his amazement. He knew a lot of the great standards and we had a pleasant chat, then, as always, at eleven, I left to my waiting taxi and went home. He came the next night. At the end of the evening he asked me if I would like to go to Sunday Jazz Brunch, at the Waldorf. I was in two minds, but I had heard of the lunches, and had wanted to go. I fought with my conscience, and decided that `lunch` would be O.K., and he had already told me he was States bound the next day so I said yes. It was very nice; he told me he was a widower. I responded.

Decades in the making

Looking out for Lil!

INTERNATIONAL singer and pianist Ruth Allen has returned to her roots, literally, by moving back to live in London after a lifetime of globetrotting, but also metaphorically because it is London which has inspired her first musical, Lil!

Allen has enjoyed a very repectable career as an artist. She was star of The Astor Club during the early fifties for a whole year, which was followed by appearances in Paris and Germany.

She married an American serviceman and virtually gave up a promising career to raise a family, although she continued entertaining the forces at air bases.

In recent years, back home in Britain, she has enjoyed something of a revival appearing in a Royal Variety Show in 1985.

Allen was born and raised in Fulham as one of a very musical family. Her brother is a respected jazz musician and their creative partnership which has endured since childhood has given rise to one of the most beautiful ballads In Love which is the pinnacle of achievement in this new work.

Lil!, a rousing musical play set in the Cockney rhyming depths of the East End, is a love story for the middle-aged which must be a first, given that most musicals hinge on the trauma of young romance.

According to Lil!, which is the story of an aged hooker and a barrow boy, love still has its traumas whatever side of 40 you happen to be on and the show, recently showcased at the Concert Artistes Association, has more plot twists than the average episode of Dallas and considerably more humour.

The title character, branded a prostitute by her father and thrown out of the house in shame, lives as a quite respectable spinster albeit as a 'loving friend' to five elderly gents, known as her 'one-a-day Mr Men,' who just happen to leave money.

Naturally, the day Lil is propositioned by Charlie the fruit vendor, is bad news for her five beaus. But the course of true love never ran smooth and Charlie and Lil split acrimoniously after he learns of the other five men in her life.

Mr Thursday, alias Donald, who actually used his time with Lil to dress up in her clothes and prefers to be known as Doris in drag, becomes the closest female friend of Lil's sister Rose and eventually her husband after revealing his penchant for crossdressing.

Of course the lovers are reunited in time for a lovely wedding down the pub and Allen could not resist the opportunity to introduce a tadge of young lurve between Lil's neice Kitty and the friendly beat bobby George who, by another freak of chance, is Charlie's brother. Happy families.

Allen has been working on the show since 1985 The idea came, quite literally she claims, in a dream. After racking her brain for a plot and characters she dreamed of a headline The Barrow Boy and The Hooker.

What developed was not a harsh piece of social comment but a gentle timeless work full of, she says, "the music that they used to write." It is a show which Allen wants punters to be able to bring the grandmother or children to see.

A US firm bought the staging option on the musical in 1987, but the deal crashed when the firm went out of business in the share slump of Black October.

She is rightly proud of her achievement and is hoping for a West End backer: "I would dearly love it to go on in London because we really need an uplift at the moment.

"We need new music. This is so singable. I can guarantee you would go away whistling the first and last number."

twinkle in their parents' eyes claims one lady magician who was around to witness it.

Claudine Harriott, now living in Manchester, will be remembered from the sixties as The Magical Claudine. Pictured above in her full glory, Claudine was billed as "dynamite, mysterious, fabulous" and "bubbling with sex appeal, colour and fun" not to mention six languages. Her father Claude Chandler was one of the most highly respected and well-loved vice presidents of the hallowed male Circle.

Given the position of father and daughter, one might have expected the young Claudine to be fighting her corner with nepotism on her side. But no. Although a feminist she may be on many issues Claudine reveals that she is 100 per cent behind the vote to keep the Magic Circle male.

Why? Well before the magiciannes scream "Cop out," Harriot points out that they are not being excluded from a rightful professional place in the entertianment business.

It is, she explains, because over 85 years the Circle has become a boys club for amateur magicians whose wives are only too happy to accept that their husdands are at the club "playing about with their bits of magic." These reassured wives might take an altogether different view if they knew that girls came with the magic too, says Harriott, and the Circle would become a place where once again men would find it hard to go without including their spouse.

A final word of advice from a hardened female pro who has been in the business, and survived it without being in the Magic Circle: "Don't spoil it for them. Leave them to their male club. Just as many a woman enjoys the Womens' Institute now I don't think she would be so happy if it became the persons' club."

Fame at last for cocktail pianist at the Savoy

by VALENTINE LOW

FOR more than 40 years Ruth Allen has been playing the jazz clubs and cocktail bars of America and Europe, eking out a living as she juggled her career with raising five children.

In her time she met Billie Holiday and turned down a chance to sing with Duke Ellington. Now in her sixties, she is the resident pianist at the American Bar at the Savoy. Today she is about to enjoy another chance of fame when two of her songs feature in new film The Real Howard Spitz, starring Frasier actor Kelsey Grammer.

Kelsey Grammer

One of the tunes, a composition titled Who Needs Spring? which she wrote with her brother 30 years ago, has been released as a single. The Savoy barman has even created a cocktail named after it. "I am pretty excited," Miss Allen said. "I can't believe it is happening."

She was rediscovered by music publisher Don Gallacher who helped her release a CD of 14 of her songs and then sent it to film companies.

Director Vadim Jean picked two songs out for the comedy, released on Friday, in which Grammer plays a crotchety children's writer who loathes children. Miss Allen said: "It was exactly what they wanted for the movie and I am really looking forward to seeing it.

"Apparently Who Needs Spring? plays on the radio in the film for more than a minute, and as much of the other music is old material, it stands out."

Ruth Allen: The Savoy's resident pianist says she "can't believe it is all happening"

Various news articles touting the talents of Ruth Allen

Decades in the making

London-born Ruth Allen's professional debut—harmonizing as one half of a singing act with a school friend—came at 15, in front of 3,000 people. Known as The Berry Sisters, the two girls collected the then princely sum of 12 pounds sterling a week between them.

Ms. Allen emerged as the accomplished cabaret artist Ronnie Graham, and she wowed audiences throughout London, most particularly at the Astor Club in Berkeley Square.

She began writing lyrics with her brother Alan Berry, an acknowledged jazz pianist. Stuck indoors on a day she would have rather have been out in the spring sunshine, she had one of Alan's melodies in her head when, out of frustration for her predicament, she announced, "Who Needs Spring?" The words and the lyrics for the song swiftly followed—except that the phrase was no longer derisory but the basis for a haunting love song.

The collaboration with her brother continued, and she also began composing her own highly memorable tunes. Almost all of her lyrics are based on events in her own life. "You're Never Too Old," for instance, is a creed she lives by, and "January Butterfly" was inspired when a beautiful butterfly appeared in her studio on a cold snowy day in January.

Ms. Allen has written a *Cockney Musical*, with 18 songs, which will be part of the Covent Garden Festival. A concert version will be presented at the Concert Association, as part of the fringe theater. It is called "Ring Out the Bow Bells."

Ms. Allen has met some wonderful people during her long and interrupted career and has missed some opportunities with no regrets. Her family, now grown, encourage her to keep going, and as long as she feels she can please people, she will.

JAZZ RELEASES *Dave Gelly*

RUTH ALLEN The Ruth Allen Songbook (*Astor AST 1112*) *In the Fifties, under the name of Ronnie Graham, Ruth Allen enjoyed a big reputation as an international cabaret singer. She returns as a singer-songwriter with this lavishly produced CD, complete with string orchestra. She has a mature, expressive voice and the kind of undemonstrative style that makes everything sound easy, even when it isn't*

The Observer Sunday 12 February 1995

Various news articles touting the talents of Ruth Allen

It was a most enjoyable lunch, and a very long one. In fact we were still there when the Tea Dance started, whereupon he asked me to dance. That was amazing as he turned out to be an excellent dancer. I hadn't had a dance partner for many years and I enjoyed it very much. It was now getting dark outside, and I said I had better be getting home. So we walked over Waterloo Bridge to look at my favourite view. It was cold, and as we stood there, he suddenly grabbed me and gave me a resounding kiss on the mouth. I was shocked, delighted, and slightly embarrassed. (It had been such a long time). I then said I must go and started walking quickly to the station to catch the train home. That was that. He left for the States the next morning.

When I arrived home, I plopped down on the sofa and hugged myself with glee, and admitted to myself how much I had really enjoyed being kissed.

That lunch turned in to the next four years while still playing at the Savoy, of letter writing and phone calls, culminating in him saying, why don't you come and live here (in New Jersey). We are both alone, it makes sense. In short, I finally I did. I was lonely and I needed a new start. I was tired of the hotel playing and I thought it would be good to make a new life. Also I would be nearer to my daughters and grandsons.

I arrived in Newark and Richard met me. My daughter and her partner were flying out to Palm Beach Florida, and we were to meet them there for a week's vacation. So we left Newark the next day and as we were flying over New York Richard pointed out of the window and I saw the twin towers in the sunlight. It was September 10th 2001.

We all met in the hotel, The Palm Beach, and had a lovely evening, retiring early. The next morning I was up making coffee when Charles came banging on the door. I opened up and he quickly said "Have you got the T.V. on" I said no, but he was already racing across the room to turn it on, at the same time saying something about a plane having crashed into one of the twin towers. At that moment Richard appeared and Gail too, and you know the rest. We were all rooted in horror. It wasn't a happy holiday. It was spent in front of the television watching the unbelievable, while outside it rained constantly. We were relieved to leave.

However, this turned out to be quite dramatic. I had left Newark to come to Florida without my passport, thinking that now I was residing in America, and travelling in America I would not need a passport. This, of course, was true before 9/11, but now everything changed. Gail and Charles and Richard and I arrived at the airport, and I was told I couldn`t leave Florida without my passport, and proof that I was a citizen of the United States. I had the necessary documents back at Richard's house of course. Gail and Charles left for London and because Richard had appointments the next day he left for Newark while I spent the rest of the day and night in a hotel by myself, explaining to Richard's Secretary where she could find the necessary paperwork to get me back to Newark. She fed-ex'd it to me so that I could leave the next day. It was slightly traumatic, especially after the terrible tragedy in New York.

Years before when my C.D. first came out, my publisher sent one to practically everyone in the "business". One was the great Michael Feinstein. Sometime later, my phone rang, and a voice said `Hello, this is Michael Feinstein speaking, is that Ruth Allen? At first I thought someone was having a joke, then I realised it was really him . . . He then said, "Someone sent me your Song Book and I just wanted to tell you I think you are a wonderful writer". I almost cried with joy! Coming from the man who oversees the Gershwin archives, it was the most tremendous compliment, probably, ever! He also said if ever I came to New York, to be sure to call him, and gave me his number.

Decades in the making

THE RUTH ALLEN SONGBOOK
VOLUME I, PAGES 1 TO 14
(ASTOR RECORDS AST 112)

Who Needs Spring? • You Took The Time • The Last Time • At Last I Have Someone • Leave Me Too My Dreams • All You Have To Do • Be A Little Devil • This Thing Called Love • Would I Still Be Me? • Only Just A Phone Call Away • Ah, But That Was A Long Time Ago • Just Knock On Any Door • You're Never Too Old • January Butterfly.

***Ruth Allen** (vocals and songs) with **Cliff Hall** (piano), **Mitch Dalton** (guitar), **Don Richardson** (bass), **Ralph Salmins** (drums), **Bob Tinker** (trumpet), **Jeff Daly** (alto sax, flute), **Dave Bitelli** (tenor sax, clarinet), **Steve Hayes** (trombone), and The London Session Orchestra, leader **Gavin Wright**. Music arranged and conducted by **Peter Thomas**, who also played all the alto, tenor saxophone and flute solos.*

Out of the 13 songs which comprise the content of this Songbook, Ruth Allen has written both words and music to 11 of them (the remaining two have music by her brother Alan Berry, with her lyrics). And there is much to commend both this lady's accomplishments: the words are neatly assembled, the dynamic stresses therein perfectly match the like nuances in the music; and I have to say she's a real dab hand at writing *tunes*. Good, memorable melodies all, with a sophistication of modulation which really does her 'middle-eights' proud.

Accompanied by a group of musicians well qualified to more than hold their own in any jazz company, and a fine string ensemble as well. The whole programme has been arranged for and conducted by Pete Thomas, who was also responsible for all the jazz solos and statements on alto and tenor saxophones and flutes—an eloquent improviser as well as an accomplished arranger. Ruth Allen, a performer of accomplishment, sings the whole songbook in a highly professional, personal way, and as a songwriter, she surely goes for Kern, Porter and a modicum of Berlin ('golden age' writers all); her songs radiate that sort of ambience and range from lenitive ballads to swingy point numbers. On the former category her voice is gentle and caressing (to a level where, I find, it may be a little *too* self-effacing, at the expense of precise, deliberate diction, but, overall, this is a minor quibble. Her treatment of the jazzier material, with its attendant insistence on clipped, self-projecting annunciation and a closer allegiance to the movements in the backing scores, is altogether a different kettle of fish, as they say, and very stylish indeed. She has obviously listened a good deal to Lena and Ella, but, of course, that can't be bad! Miss Allen, an artiste of vast experience in cabaret both here and in the States, is a talent to be reckoned with, and has a courage to be admired (I note the label is 'Astor Records', and, noting she once held a year's residence at London's chic Astor Club in Berkeley Square—has she funded this project herself?). An estimable effort. Next time, Ruth, how about a little more of that intimate jazz style you accomplish so well?

Ken Rattenbury

Various news articles touting the talents of Ruth Allen

Decades in the making

CAA

The Empty Theatre

This "supernatural variety extravaganza," conceived by Ruth Allen, is proof that sometimes the simplest ideas can produce the most pleasurable of theatrical experiences.

For those who love to revel in a bit of nostalgia, The Empty Theatre, co-directed by Michael Garland and Bruce Douglas, is the perfect opportunity to remember some of the great artists of old.

George (Douglas) finds himself back in the venue where he once worked, which is now just an empty shell, except for a basket of old props and costumes. Throughout the show he picks items out, each symbolising a different performer, and bringing their ghosts alive for one last time. As they appear, whether it be Marie Lloyd (Bettina Raymond), Lady Tree (Susan Travers) or Evelyn Laye (Elizabeth Winton), Douglas sets the scene by telling a little of their life stories as well.

The rest of the delightful cast includes Ronnie Joyce, June Lewis, Audrey Joyce, Marcia Lindon, Glen Hayes and Jules Mannheim. Mary Morland may be 79 years old, but she still has a glorious singing voice, while Garland impressed with a rapid rendition of a song from Iolanthe.

But I must say the highlight of the evening is probably Mike Mayes as Stanley Holloway. If there was a dry eye in the house after he had sung Brahn Boots I would be very much surprised.

Piano accompaniment came from Ronnie Bridges and on other nights is provided by Mary

news

MICHAEL FEINSTEIN PRESENTS "NOW AND THEN" AT CARNEGIE HALL

Michael Feinstein - pianist-singer and world renowned advocate of the great songwriters is to present a special show at Carnegie Hall in New York City on December 6th. Michael - a long-time admirer of Ruth Allen's work - asked the producer especially to book Ruth.

The program will feature five 'new' composers performing one each of their own songs as well as paying tribute to the great songwriter Charles Strouse.

"NOW & THEN" THURSDAY DECEMBER 6TH 2001 at the WEILL RECITAL HALL, CARNEGIE HALL, NEW YORK CITY, N.Y.
Presented by MICHAEL FEINSTEIN and featuring
RUTH ALLEN - JEFF FRANZEL - DAVID GANON - SALLY MAYES - ADRYAN RUSS

Check out http://www.carnegiehall.org for more details

RUTH TO PERFORM IN BRITISH GALA CHARITY BENEFIT - NEW YORK CITY!

Ruth, after only five weeks in the States, has been asked to perform at a Gala Benefit in aid of the families of the 239 British people who died in the World Trade Center disaster on September 11th.

Titled "FROM PICCADILLY TO TIMES SQUARE" the show is on Monday November 19th at the New York Historical Society.

Ruth will be in the company of fellow artists Natasha Richardson, Hayley Mills, George Shearing, Donna McKechnie and Carmen Lavallade.

"From Piccadilly To Times Square"
The New York Historical Society - 2 West 17th Street / Central Park West.
Monday 19th November 2001. Please check for times and ticket availability.

As I Was Saying . . Jan 25 198– Falmouth Enterprise

Singer Here Has Made It Big In England

by Hugh R. McCartney

Just some idle reflections cast in a blue indigo mood, mostly about the smiling man who sat in the corner at the piano.

They met in a small pub in London recently. He was over there on Westinghouse business. His name was Rudy. He blew tenor sax on the Cape for a while about 30 years ago when he was stationed at Otis.

He couldn't take his eyes off the torch singer. There was something vaguely familiar about her, the face and the voice that told all there was to tell about life the way it really is. A sax man knows these things.

She had no problems jumping back and forth between the cockney delivery for the natives and the throaty, definitely American voice she used on the blues numbers.

They talked after the set was over.

"You must have spent some time in the U.S.," Rudy said to her.

"Yeh, I did. I was on Cape Cod," the woman told him. She said her name was Ronnie Halpern but she sometimes goes by the name Graham.

"Really? I was on Cape Cod for a while too. I was stationed at Otis," Rudy said.

"You're kidding. My husband was stationed at Otis," Ronnie said, adding, "I loved the Cape. I used to sing at a place called Tanya's and a few others. We had a good group. A guy, Frank Smaller, played the piano, and we had the best guitar player on the Cape."

"Oh no. Our group had the best guitar player on the Cape over at the base officer's club," Rudy protested, "named Souza."

"You played with George Souza too? How about that," Ronnie said.

See, Rudy called the Falmouth shellfish warden-guitar player a while back and told him this story. Ronnie has gone big time and even cut a record.

"I ordered one. I couldn't wait to play it for Frank. You know, those last few weeks, all he had was memories. The record finally arrived."

"When?" George was asked.

"Last Wednesday. The day of the funeral."

Various news articles touting the talents of Ronnie Graham aka Ruth Allen

So, now living in New Jersey, as soon as I could I called, and left a message. I later received a message from Michael's Manager that said Michael has a show coming up to honour Charles Strouse the song-writer, and present four new song-writers. Michael Feinstein insists you be in the show. It`s at Carnegie Hall, on December 6th 2001." Believe me, it was one of the greatest highlights of my life! I also took part in a great benefit show for the Brits who died in 9/11. The top artist on this show was none other than the great George Shearing. I thought I was "IN" . . . . .

But to be "in" meant living in New York and at this particular time it was out of the question. I had only just arrived in Point Pleasant, New Jersey, and you need a lot of money to live in New York. I soon made friends, and Richard's sister Ginny, was wonderful, and very kind. I felt very welcome but, even so, I did not like the house Richard lived in. It had been his marital home, although his wife had been dead for many years, and they were divorced even before she died. I knew it was irrational, but I just couldn`t bring myself to feel really comfortable. Richard, I came to find out, never threw anything away. Not for sentimental reasons, but he didn't even think about it.

Carnegie Hall

The Best Night of My Life
December 6, 2001

Michael Feinstein &
Ruth Allen

CARNEGIE HALL

The 2001–2002 season is dedicated to the legacy of Isaac Stern, who led Carnegie Hall for more than 40 years with uncompromising determination, passion, generosity, and wisdom.

Thursday Evening, December 6, 2001, at 8:00
Weill Recital Hall

CARNEGIE HALL PRESENTS

THE BEST NIGHT OF MY LIFE: CELEBRATING THE SONGS OF CHARLES STROUSE

MICHAEL FEINSTEIN, *Artistic Director and Host*

STARRING:
RUTH ALLEN
JEFF FRANZEL
DAVID GANON
ADRYAN RUSS

WITH SPECIAL GUESTS:
SALLY MAYES
SHARON MCNIGHT
MARY STOUT

The program will be announced from the stage.

There will be one intermission.

Made possible by a generous grant from The Alice Tully Foundation.

Additional support is provided by The DuBose and Dorothy Heyward Memorial Fund and The Blanche and Irving Laurie Foundation.

Produced for Carnegie Hall by Michael A. Kerker/ASCAP.

Review of Ruth Allen & Alan Berry's CD entitled, Head to Head

I first heard Ruth Allen sing in the Pine Bar of the Britannia Hotel in Mayfair, one of those unadvertised West-End spots (the Savoy is her present Friday night venue) where the cognoscenti unwind in her tuneful company after hours. I admired her warmth and professionalism as she accompanied herself on piano that night, and here she has the luxury of a piano trio led by her brother Alan Berry, a respected player and composer on th London scene, behind her.

Together Ruth and Alan have produced an album of 16 new British songs, written and performed with the quality of an age when popular music meant much more than the disposable trash that dominates our radio-waves today. Their specialty is the ambience where jazz and cabaret coincide, an adult area for listeners who have outgrown the adolescent "I wantcha to be my babyee" lyrics of disco-land and don't have time for slushy moon-June pap. These are intelligent songs with thoughtful lyrics and adventurous melodies – Lines to test any singer. The brisk bossa-nova Can it be Love, for instance, has some difficult leaps in its melody line, as does the graceful waltz Mine Alone, but Ruth negotiates them as sure-footedly as a mountain gazelle. Alan contributes three instrumentals – Indigo, Funny Little Woman, and Moonleaves – to the session and some typically elegant keyboard work throughout, including a synthesizer solo on the witty, up-tempo cautionary tale, Say Hi to Julie. My favourite number, the medium-paced ballad All Over Again, has such a natural line that it could be an old standard. It's not, though, it's totally original, another classy combination of Alan's music and Ruth's lyrics. Lonely Man of Malmo, a late-night tale of a solitary businessman a long way from home, is a lyric with the insight only a seasoned piano-bar entertainer like Ruth could have. In a more enlightened world she and her brother would be working to much larger audiences. Who knows, it could still happen. But until it does, albums as well-crafted as this are hard to find.

Congratulations on getting your hands on a copy.
It's going to give you a lot of pleasure, not just next week or next year, but for years to come. That's what quality means.

Jack Massarik
(Jazz critic, London evening Standard)

Quote from the Legendary David Jacobs from his
BBC Radio 2 Broadcast,
"The David Jacobs Collection" March 10, 2013

"Although she's not all that well known,
the London born cabaret artist Ruth Allen
has a very important place in the Collection
having performed at the Astor Club in
Berkeley Square, the American Bar at the Savoy Hotel,
and goodness knows where else.
It is only right she should become better known,
not just as a performer but as a composer,
for she's written many lovely songs,
more than a dozen of which she performs
on a CD called, *The Ruth Allen Songbook.*"

David Jacobs
March 2013

I had left the house I loved, and most of my belongings, and I guess I resented the fact that nothing had changed for him, except that he now had a live-in partner. Richard had been a bachelor for twenty or more years, and here I was expecting him to change just like that . . . . Well of course he couldn`t. It was very difficult to live with a man like this, and I wondered where I actually fitted in. Was I just a trophy to hang on his arm? Was I just useful? I was not happy.

Because my house in England was rented for a year, I had nowhere to go, so I decided to make the best of it. Our social life was great and I enjoyed dressing up and going to the Golf Club of which he was a member. I played the piano there and met a lot of lovely people. We also threw some wonderful parties which were very popular. It was still hard to live with Richard on a day-to-day basis though. He was so un-bending in his lifestyle, but I had to fit in with his.

I became a volunteer at the local hospital as I had in Utah. There was an electric piano in the entrance hall (called the Atrium) and every Wednesday morning from 9am until 12noon, I would play and sing to the patients and people coming in for one-day surgery. There was another lady that played on Monday too. Everyone loved it, and I did too. It gave me practice and enjoyment, and a much needed other dimension. I was known as the Musical Therapist.

The life at home was not good though. I hated his house, it had been the marital home and was full of his late wife`s things and memories. The only good thing was that I had my own bedroom and bathroom. I did not feel loved at all. I felt more like a trophy, to be shown off to all his friends. I blame myself entirely for letting this happen. It is unexplainable even to me. There were some good times of course, but the bad days were overtaking them. I had to admit to myself I was miserable and homesick. I had made many really wonderful friends and they all knew it. My daughters were not happy either and thought I should get out. There has to come a right time though, and when it comes you know . . . . And I knew . . . .

Eight years prior, my daughter Gail and her partner Charles Garside, had bought a hotel in the Lake District called, "MILLER HOWE". The first time I went there, I fell in love. It is the most beautiful place, only 15 rooms, and all of it beautiful. When I had decided to go to the States to live with Richard, I gave them my beautiful grand piano to put in the hotel where it looked so splendid in one of the lounges—Like it was born there. My daughter Beth and I spent three Christmases there entertaining with Gail joining in. Wonderful and memorable times, and for the customers as well, who used to call ahead to make sure we were going to be there.

This then was where I wanted to be. My house in London was rented. Charles is now the Managing Editor of The Daily Mail, as well as owning the hotel, and their cottage adjacent to the Hotel, was empty most of the time. At my plaintive plea, could I reside at the cottage, I would like to play for the hotel. They said they thought it would be a good idea. I love them very much.

The time I spent at the cottage was invaluable to getting me, myself, and my soul back. I spent many, many hours with the rain and my own thoughts as company, something I had never really done as I had always been married and with children, etc., and as every Mum knows, unconsciously, your thoughts about yourself, your needs, your wants, etc. get pushed to the back of the closet, so to speak, until, sometimes, you forget they are there. This reflective time, this blessing, although very lonely at times, was good for me. A healing time. I needed it. So, after two years of battling with myself and my thoughts I was finally getting on with it, getting used to it, re-inventing myself, playing and singing again, meeting people, enjoying myself and my own company, as it were, and actually starting to feel like myself again when I received a phone call . . . . It was Richard. We talked at length. He begged for me to come back. He apologized for how things hadn't materialized the way he said they would, and asked me for another chance. Along with that discussion came word he had been diagnosed with lung cancer and now this once boisterous, quirky, funny, unbending, decisive, opinionated, strong, elephant-in-a-china-closet of a man was vulnerable and scared and didn't want to go it alone. I couldn't blame him for that and after much grappling with myself and my kids, I knew I wouldn't be able to live with myself if I let him finish his days alone. I finally decided, against everyone's thoughts and wishes on the matter, to stuff my feelings back in the closet and return to New Jersey.

My arrival was joyous! Richard was jubilant, and it was wonderful to see all my friends again. Richard had told me upon my return that we could redecorate\update the house to more of my liking, so he and I began picking out new furniture, had the walls painted with colour, etc. Once he saw the difference these small changes made he said he loved it and wondered why he hadn't done it years ago—go figure. However, it was not long before the absolute drudgery of the whole situation came to light and was staring me in the face, again, day-in and day out. The same old existence, only this time Richard was ill, very ill, which made it all the worse. Over the next eighteen months it became a 24 hour/7 day-a-week care situation that made us both housebound. Help eventually had to be called in as I just couldn't cope with it all—all by myself. It was a gruelling, tortuous time watching cancer slowly take Richard away while standing by helplessly watching the life slowly drain out of this very proud man. So much sadness. Richard was laid to rest in February 2007.

As the reader will by now have realised, very unusual surprises often crop up when we least expect it. I received a phone call from my daughter Gail who lives in England. From the sound of her voice I could tell she was very excited about something . . . .

"Mum, You will never believe what happened. I ran into an old friend that I hadn`t seen for ten years. We used to work together on the European Newspaper. He and his wife are great people. We went to a near-by pub to chat and catch up. Of course he asked about you and I told him you were living back in the States and went on to say you were still singing and playing, and had written a musical called RING OUT THE BOW BELLS. He looked at me so strangely and said, do you mean the church called ST. MARY LE BOW? Yes I said and he beamed and told me that his very best friend was the administrator of the church. How incredible is that? It was amazing! When we arranged to meet again he said he would take me to the church and meet his dear friend Nick.

We were so welcomed and had lunch in the crypt of this magnificent, and centuries old church, parts of which are a thousand years old! It has been destroyed three times, the last time in world war two, but it always was rebuilt and has survived . . . How wonderful.

Gail then went on to say that Nick was intrigued by the show and said it ought to put it on right here, at the church! What an incredible idea. To actually perform your Musical in the church that inspired it. To say I was delighted was putting it mildly. So the next thing I knew I was winging it back to London to meet this lovely man and see this beautiful church. It was everything and more than Gail had told me. It even had a very wide alter the width of the church, which would make a beautiful stage.

Once again I rallied my wonderful friends at the C.A.A. and soon had a cast, and a director, who the last time we did the play was my leading man, ha. It was a lot of really hard work even though we did a wonderful concert version. The singing was sublime and the acting marvellous. The greatest people I have ever met. We had fliers made to advertise and even got a London beer company to sponsor us. It was, of course, performed to make some much needed money for the churches various charities. After the show we all drank beer in the lobby and sang the opening and closing number, RING OUT THE BOW BELLS. My daughters Beth and Gail and their cousin Paula all took part in the chorus . . . . It was truly a marvellous night and to crown it all, they called in the bell-ringers on opening night, and the sound is something you can never forget. Of course as the legend tells it if you were born within the sound of the bow bells, you are a true-blue cockney . . . . That night we all were.

I still am awestruck to think this all happened because of a chance meeting of two old friends. Life is beautiful, my cup runneth over. I feel very blessed. I only hope that someday, somehow, the whole show will be seen and heard. Everyone who saw it that night in the church LOVED it, but we didn`t land any millionaire investors sooooooooo, the dream lives on—any takers???

2012

It has taken many, many years—a lifetime to be exact, and a lot of getting used to, but I have finally come to terms with so many issues, concerns, and events that have happened in my life. I am more at peace with myself than I have ever been, and although not completely sold on the idea, I can be happy living on my own. I have recently moved from the East Coast to the West Coast (better on the bones and closer to my daughter) and have a beautiful home in Southern California. I am blessed with excellent health, youthful looks, and the opportunity each day to spend the day doing whatever I want, whenever I want and with whoever I want—definitely something to be said for that. Sure, I get lonely and I feel very blue at times, but I've learned everybody does, and that's ok. Just keep moving. Truth be told, I am still very much an old school romantic at heart, meaning I haven't thrown out the possibility another Mr. Right could come a knockin'. But until he does, or even if he doesn't, I will survive and thrive knowing I am surrounded by the most wonderful, caring friends, and loving family anyone could ask for.

As I finish writing this book I continue to be a Musical Therapist, playing and singing at a wonderful assisted living facility in town. With a healthy family and many, many caring, wonderful friends that I know will always be there, I really have all that I need; the rest is up to me. One of my lyrics comes to mind. It has become my theme song—"You're Never too old to be you, cause deep down inside you're the same old you. Stop thinking that your done is done. You haven't finished till the game is won." ..It is so true; the trick's not to die, till you do.

I am winning this game called life and living and loving every minute of it. Through it all though . . . . I'll Still Be Me. ☺.

Who Needs Spring

Music: Alan Berry Lyric: Ruth Allen

My brother wrote this lovely tune and I wrote the lyric. It remains one of our favourites and one of the first collaborations.

Who needs Spring to fall in love?
All I need is you.
Who needs lambs and daffodils and swings.

What's so great that flowers can't wait
To flirt with butterflies
All year long there's springtime in your eyes.

Winter, love is warm,
Summer, 'bove norm
Fall, I fall again.

So Who Needs Spring to fall in love?
Who needs skies of blue?
I don't need a season, I need you.

I don't need a season, I need you.

<u>You Took The Time</u>

Words and Music: Ruth Allen

This song and its inspiration is also mentioned in the Memoirs. I was surprised and pleased with this song, and I love the arrangement too.

<u>Verse</u>

I was never a whiz in the city, disappointed my Mum and Dad
And I certainly wasn't witty; wit was something I never had
And so I grew up thinking I must be dumb
But always blindly hoping there was more to com . . . . then . . . .

You took the time and the trouble just to find me
You took the time, and the effort to unwind me
You stopped to smell the fragrance, and found the perfume
Turned candlelight to radiance, dispelling the gloom
Your silent smile was an eloquent mime
I'm so glad that, You Took The Time

You took the time, just to dig a little deeper
You took the time, and discovered a deep sleeper
I'm better stirred not shaken, you found the right spoon
So eager to awaken, you played the right tune
You knocked, but I heard a bell start to chime
I'm so glad that, You Took The Time.

You took the time, and you made me a believer
You took the time, now my heart is the receiver
You listened to the whispers and heard shouts of joy
You looked right through the shadows, and saw the real McCoy
You saved me from that long uphill climb
I'm so glad that, You Took The Time

For this Jill, Jack, you made the nursery rhyme!!
I'm so glad that, YOU TOOK THE TIME . . . .

The Last Time

Words and Music: Ruth Allen

The inspiration for this song came from meeting my late husband, Geoffrey. I had known Geoff since childhood and we hadn't see each other for twenty-five years. I had been playing in hotels in Europe and all over for many years. Don, my publisher at the time, had been saying, "write something simple". Well, it doesn't get much simpler than this. I think this would suite a country and western artist . . . .

Verse
I've travelled the world on my own
I've never needed love
Till on a visit back home
I found what I've never dreamed of . . .

A love that was to last, was the last thing on my mind,
Till I fell in love with you
I was unprepared for the harmony we shared
And I knew you cared for me too.

You looked into my eyes, and to my surprise
I felt butterflies inside
All my worldly ways, were lost within your gaze,
For my world was there in your eyes.

A love that was to last, was the last thing on my mind
Till I fell in love with you
We fell in love for the first time
And the last time too . . . .

At Last I Have Someone

Words and Music: Ruth Allen

This song was inspired by my late husband. It describes the way he influenced me and the way I enjoyed our life together.

AT LAST I HAVE SOMEONE I can laugh with
Be a child with, someone who makes me shine
At last I no longer feel the sadness
Just the gladness, now you are mine

You have turned the world around for me
I can see the other side
You have whirled me round till I am free
To enjoy the fun of every ride

At last I have someone I'm in love with
Want to be with every moment of my time
The loneliness has passed, we are together
Forever, at last . . . .

Leave Me To My Dreams

Words and Music: Ruth Allen

Reading a book about an actor I had admired for years, one of those so-called exposés. I became angry—how dare someone try to destroy my illusions. What did I care of his private fancies. I had hoped to read about his greatness, and his career, only to find myself being turned into a voyeur. I threw the book away and am since very careful about the things I read . . . .

Verse

I suppose you could call me naïve
I only believe what I want to believe
I'm so much happier this way
Spare me another exposé, please

Leave me to my dreams; it's where I'd rather be
I don't wish to know the whys and wherefore
Leave my dreams alone, hands off my illusions
Reality is something I don't care for

Books that are written telling all
Are books I won't be reading
Turning heroes into fools
Are tools I won't be needing

Leave me to my dreams I'll view the world through moonbeams
At least I'll know those moon dreams are mine
Be still that eager pen
Some day, maybe I'll want to see
But leave me to my dreams till then . . . .

All You Have to Do

Words and Music: Ruth Allen

Staying in California with my wonderful kids. They gave me the idea for this lyric. Whenever they had to leave me alone in the house, they would always impress upon me "All you have to do Mom, if you need anything, anything at all, just call me and I'll be here in no time." "Don't Forget Mom, that's all you have to do."

Verse

Whether I'm pounding keyboards
Washing floorboards
Or just keeping scoreboards
I love you, I love you . . . . and . . . .

All you have to do, is love me in return
Then I'll be sure that I'll be loved forever
All you have to say is I am here to stay
And we will always be together

All the I desire, is in your every smile
Just to look at you is to adore you
All you have to be is waiting here for me
Forever and a day I'll be here for you

For I am absolutely certain
That I would never change at all
And if you're absolutely certain
You'll be my Summer, Winter, Spring, and Fall

All you have to do, is love me in return
Then I'll be sure that I'll be loved forever
Let me hear you say, I love you, everyday,
And we will always be . . . . together . . . .

Be A Little Devil

Words & Music: Ruth Allen

I am very pleased with this song. The idea came from being out for a drink with friends. Towards the end of the evening, and saying, "no thanks" to a last drink, someone would inevitably say, "Oh, go on, be a little devil", and I would inevitably say, "Oh, alright then". Ha. Once the idea took root, it took me a very short time to write the whole song. It fell right into place, words and music almost simultaneously. It is soooooooo much fun when that happens–not too often. My brother said when I first sang it to him, "Where did that come from then?" I told him it was a surprise to me too. Though it is somewhat difficult to sing, children love it!

Be a little devil
And tell me on the level that you love me
That you really love me
You, I dare

Gettin' kinda hazy, I'm
Tired of picking petals off a daisy
And the daisy's not too crazy
It's feeling bare

There must be an ending to this stalemate
I need a male mate, my dear that's you
So, before I reach my sell-by-date
Come on and seal my fate
Say I love you

Turn into an angel
I think maybe the change'll make a difference
Say the magic words
So I can say I love you too

Be a little devil, tell me that you love me too . . . .

This Thing Called Love

Words and Music: Ruth Allen

Cole Porter has always had my complete admiration. A consummate song-writer. I have been singing his marvellous songs for most of my life, and never get tired of them. One of his famous songs is, of course, WHAT IS THIS THING CALLED LOVE. So here in my song I have tried to answer his question. Whether I succeeded or not is for the listener to decide. I did so enjoy writing it. I love singing it too.

Verse
A long time ago a Mr. Cole Porter wrote
What is this thing called love
So I sorta pondered the question
And I found the answer
By falling in love myself . . .

It's his eyes that tell me that I'm beautiful
And mine let him know that he's divine
It's his mind that seems so inscrutable
That mystery, that makes me toe the line

It's his sense of humour that I find such fun
It's my laugh that warms him through and through
It's his arms so cozy when there's not much sun
For a love like that there's nothing I won't do

It's his masculinity that makes me so female
It's my femininity that makes him a he-male
With sharing and caring and guidance from above
That, Mr. Porter, is this thing called love

It's his kind of honesty that I admire
It's my open heart that he adores
It's my kind of chemistry makes him perspire
It's his kisses that arouse encores

It's his footsteps that I always listen for
It's my very understanding ways
It's my smile that greets him at our own front door
We're trapped for the rest of our days

It's his kind of living that makes me so loving
It's our kind of loving that makes life worth living

With sharing and caring and guidance from above
That, Mr. Porter is, this thing called love . . . .

Would I Still Be Me

Music and Lyrics: Ruth Allen

This is one of the songs from my show. My leading lady, LIL, is thinking aloud of her life, of her Mother who had died in her child-birth, and her Father who had all her life blamed her and kicked her out when she became pregnant herself. When, in the show, she sings this song, she is middle-aged and living alone. She had miscarried in her youth, and never married. Her sister and a niece she never knew she had, have unexpectedly arrived, and she is preparing to tell her newly found niece about her life. It has been over twenty years since she last saw her sister . . . .

Would I still be me?
If he'd had a change of heart
If I'd had a different start
Would I still be me?

Happy to be free
Even though I must belong
Life has taught me right from wrong
And still I'm me

I tried to change the way things were
But it was a disguise
I'd look into a mirror
And I'd see me . . . in my eyes

There will always be
An empty space to fill
And perhaps I never will
Find that place to be . . . .
But I'll still be . . . . .me . . . .

Only Just a Phone Call Away

Music: Alan Berry   Lyric: Ruth Allen

It's the unexpectedness of sudden inspiration that continues to fascinate me. For instance, I was visiting my daughter Lynn in Utah and bemoaning the fact that I lived so far away, which prevented me from visiting more often and she said, "Oh Mom, you're only just a phone call away". Magic! I had this tune from Alan that I liked so much, and suddenly knew it would fit. It also reminded me of the countless hours I have waited for THAT phone call that may change my life, or at least my job.

Verse

Anticipation . . . . is the wellspring of us all
Especially when you are waiting for that call . . . .

The telephone when it rings
All the hope that it brings
That dies inside, like a bird robbed of wings
The questions and the answers I had ready to say,
They are only just a phone call away

I sit and stare a the phone
Wondering, are you alone?
Afraid to know I just stay on my own
And wish that I could find the words
The right words to say,
For you're only just a phone call away.

Only a moment in time, a mechanical chime
That would change into the sound of your voice
I'd be emotional, declare my love
For darling, I'm left with no other choice.

So, I uncradle the phone
Hoping you are alone
To hear the words that will make you my own
The love that was to change my life this day
The love . . . . That was only just a phone call away.

Ah, But That Was A Long Time Ago

Words and Music: Ruth Allen

Thinking back to the days of courting. Before kids and responsibilities. When going out with someone special was so romantic. It really was 'a long time ago' but lovely to look back on. Guess I am a romantic at heart. Nothing wrong with that!!

Eyes meeting eyes through a candle flame
Mind greeting mind, thoughts the same
Thrill finding thrill, as fingers touch
Need reaching need, wanting too much
Oh, the passion and the glow,
Ah, but that was a long time ago.

Soft is the sigh that hides a madly throbbing heart
Still are the hands that long to explore
Quiet, is the space, holding us apart
Bright are the eyes you adore . . .

Time passes by and heals the pain
Leaving a heart free to love again
Now with the wisdom years provide
With a smile so softening the pride
Never should have let him go
Ah, but that was a long time ago . . . .

Just Knock On Any Door

Music: Alan Berry Words: Ruth Allen

Alan actually named this himself, before he played it to me. What a great title. It really got me thinking. Then he added, "When you've got the blues" Wow, I thought, this is great! So, with all this help I set to work. I think it is a really good song, and I'm proud of it.

Just knock on any door when you've got the blues
Just knock on any door any one you choose
Just take a look inside and you will see
That the blues you've got, has some company

Just knock on any door when you're feeling down
Just knock on any door anywhere in town
It's just the same on both sides of the track
That's life; there ain't no looking back . . .

'Cause people everywhere, need people everywhere . . . . who care
That is something you can't buy
But when it comes to love, remember the good Lord above
And find a soul that's blue, who'll split the blues with you

Just knock on any door, anywhere on earth
Just knock on any door, and you'll find it's worth
More than all of the treasures in the world and so much more . . . .

So let's begin, shout a welcome, come on in
When somebody knocks on your door
When somebody . . . . Knocks on your door

You're Never Too Old

Words and Music: Ruth Allen

The last line of this song was written in an essay by my son, Paul, when he was attending college. I might add he received a big fat "A" too. I was so proud of him he would have been a great writer. You're Never Too Old is a very popular phrase these days, especially when you can do so much to disguise it. Ha. I try to live by this philosophy. It is also featured in my show, with the two sisters singing and dancing to it. It worked very well.

Verse

Should you hear yourself saying, "Gosh, how I wish"
And thinking that life's passed you by
Get off your caboose, and shake yourself loose
Anything can happen if you try . . . .

You're never too old to re-new
For deep down inside, you're the same old you
Stop thinking that your done is done
You haven't finished till the game is won

You're never too old to relate
You'll only lose if you hesitate
Tell old Father Time to get lost!
But for safety keep your fingers crossed

Like an old house with new central heating
The warmth inside of you takes some beating
Age only shows on the outside
So revive what's alive on the inside . . . .

You're never too old to get smart
It can never be too late to start again
To Thine Own Self Be True
The trick's not to die till you do!
And you're never too old to be you . . . .

January Butterfly

Words and Music: Ruth Allen

I think this is probably my best song. It is a true story that happened one January day when the ground was covered with a light covering of snow. A Monarch Butterfly appeared in my husband's studio. He caught is in his hands and rushed downstairs to show me this wondrous thing. It flew off and landed on the window sill, and with the snow visible outside, we took a picture of it. It lived with us for ten days, and disappeared as it had arrived, without a trace. It took me along time to write this song to my satisfaction, and then I realised the words had become an analogy of my own life, without any awareness at all when I was writing it. I think it was a gift from my son . . . .

Verse

Alone in my studio, a sudden movement caught my eye,
And much to my amazement, I saw a golden butterfly

January Butterfly, where have you been hibernating?
Have you just been hiding waiting
To defy the winter snow

January Butterfly, seeking warmth around my ceiling
Weaving patterns so appealing
Like a penny picture show

Like you, I've been hiding biding my time
Afraid of life and what it brings
But now, I feel the urge to emerge and fly with you
On your golden wings

January Butterfly, you have been an inspiration
I am filled with admiration,
For your courage and your style

I'll remember you forever
And in remembering I'll smile
January, hurry by,
For I know that I can fly

Like My Butterfly.

Nothing's Changed

Words and Music: Ruth Allen

This is the song I was asked to write especially for the Royal Variety Show, which was held in 1985 at the Birmingham Hippodrome called, "Oh, What a Lovely Peace", and attended by Her Royal Highness, Princess Anne. It was the only original song in the show, and accompanied a sketch by Trevor Handoll. It depicted a soldier returning from the war who had been separated from his wife and children for five years. Stuck somewhere in Burma, the forgotten army. He is from the north of England, tired and disillusioned he arrives back to his old neighbourhood.

Verse
As I turn the corner of this miserable old street
Memories come flooding back again.
There's the same faint smell of cabbage,
That lingers in the air
Empty milk-bottles, the copper on the beat
The same old twitching curtains
The dust-bins by the steps
I know that I am back again
To fish and chips and . . . . .depts.

Nothing's Changed,
Oh, I'm glad to be alive, and I can't wait to see my Kate, but
Nothing's Changed
Thank God we all survived all the horror and the hate
But Nothing's Changed

Don't know what I expected, but it all seems somehow smaller
Can't wait to see the kids, at least I know they'll be much taller
But Kate, will she still want me, it's been so long this rotten war
Six long years of misery, and what's it all been for?
Nothing's changed . . . .

So here I am, at last I'm home, and I see there in their eyes
The love I've missed all these long years, and I realise

Nothing's Changed . . . .
I can feel the love around me that I left so long ago, no
Nothing's Changed
Their laughter now surrounds me shutting out the grief and woe, no
Nothing's Changed
We'll pick up all the pieces, we owe it to the others
Those who didn't make it back again to wives and kids and Mothers

And although we'll count the awful cost, we're free to live in Blighty
Think of the hell, if we had lost, then thank the Great Almighty
NOTHING'S CHANGED, NOTHING'S CHANGED, NOTHING'S CHANGED . . . .

Ray and Barb, very dear friends of Mum,
were sitting around chatting one day about Ruth
and her music and original songs and suddenly
as if to write itself, the song titles started coming together
into this wonderful tribute to the very talented Ruth Allen.....

Just a Quick Hello from Esher
And
a Tribute to Our Friend Ruth.

Who needs (What?)

Who needs Spring?, when I already have a January Butterfly.
The Last Time, I spoke to you, I was Only Just a Phone Call Away,
but At Last, I Have Someone, (Ah, But That Was a Long Time Ago).
You Took The Time to say, You're Never Too Old,
but don't Just Knock On Any Door, knock on mine.

I know I can Be a Little Devil, but if I changed, Would I Still Be Me?,
and anyway, What Is This Thing called Love?.
All You Have To Do, is, Leave Me To My Dreams.

Best Wishes,
Ray & Barb in Surrey, England.
August 2013

THANK YOU

THANK YOU

THANK YOU

Although there are many people throughout
my life that have left permanent
impressions on the blueprint of my life
I must take a moment to recognize and
acknowledge some very special people.
It is with every fiber of my very being
that I give my most heart-felt thanks
to the people listed below for their dedication
to this labor of love and for making it possible
for me to check another item off my "bucket list".
Much love and thank you to all of you. Cheers!

Concert Artists Association (CAA)
Beth Allen (aka Baby Ruth)
Charles & Gail Garside
Robyn Mansfield
Michael Feinstein
Ray & Barbara Probert

I am grateful to God for my wonderful family
My three daughters, Gail, Beth and Lynn
and my sons Paul and Greg

And a special thank you to my fabulous brother Alan Berry

For information please check out www.ruth-allen.com

Who would have thought I had it in me? A little girl from Fulham, England. I have been an entertainer most all of my life as a singer/pianist, and also a songwriter, but I never had any ambition to write a Musical whatsoever. I'd never even thought of such a thing until one night at the Pine Bar (best known piano-bar in London at the time).
I was playing one of Alan's tunes that I'd put words to called, "In Love", a beautiful ballad, and when I'd finished a lady came over and asked me what show the song was from. I thanked her and told her it was "one of ours" and that was that until the same thing happened again and again on different nights. People thought my songs, mine and Alan's songs, were from a show! It made me wonder - what sort of show would they be from? Writing "Ring Out The Bow Bells" was a total joy for me. I am still amazed - a full blown Musical! The Concert Artistes Association located on Bedford Street, where I am a member, put on a concert version of the show and it was amazing! Their generosity of spirit and talent was overwhelming. I will never forget them and how gratifying it was to hear my songs being sung, and my words being said... for love...Angel, are you out there?

www.ruth-allen.com

Lightning Source UK Ltd.
Milton Keynes UK
UKOW04n1933251114

242154UK00002B/24/P

9 781491 851937